WORSHIP
INTERACTIVE

WORSHIP INTERACTIVE

24 services for all-age worship

Michael Forster

kevin mayhew

First published in 2002 by
KEVIN MAYHEW LTD
Buxhall, Stowmarket, Suffolk IP14 3BW
E-mail: info@kevinmayhewltd.com

9 8 7 6 5 4 3 2 1 0

ISBN 1 84003 900 0
Catalogue No 1500502

Cover design by Angela Selfe
Edited by Katherine Laidler
Typesetting by Louise Selfe
Printed in Great Britain

Contents

Foreword

The all-age services in this book have been adapted from the *Three + One* Junior Church material, and are offered here as an alternative for those whose need is for stand-alone services without the Junior Church link.

The basic principle remains the same, though: they're meant to be truly all-age, addressing the needs of adults as well as children, and they're intended to involve people actively in the working out of the themes.

Although no longer directly linked to Junior Church, they obviously still lend themselves to a co-operative approach. So, while it would usually be possible for one person to take the whole responsibility for preparing and leading the services, it would be even better to involve, say, the youth organisations in the preparation work. A leader might get quite an interesting response from a youth club by saying, 'We need a prison cell erected in the church for the next family service'!

As with the *Three + One* series, story-telling is the basis of the material. I continue to be convinced that the best way of helping faith to grow is by telling stories – stories that engage the imagination and the emotions as well as the intellect; we are a story-telling community, with a great wealth of history to share. Most often, the stories and the activities will provide all the 'teaching' needed; the talk can then be short and to the point. Don't omit it entirely too often, though – listening is a good discipline for Christians of all ages to learn!

Each story also has a dramatised version, which, if appropriate, could be given to a children's organisation in advance for them to present in the service in place of the narrative.

Festooned (as C. S. Lewis would have said) around the stories are other vital elements of worship – praise, confession, intercession, and so on – because worship must always be more than *just* any one thing. I hope these resources may enable churches, as living, relating communities, to offer as much of their lives as they know to God.

Shalom

Michael Forster

God calls his people

God's promise and call to Abraham _____

Preparation page

What's the point?

God's promise came first, and his love for Abram was unconditional, but in order to receive what God promised, Abram had to respond freely. God wouldn't just force his way on him. So God promised (grace) and Abraham responded (faith). Similarly, God won't force himself upon us, and neither will he magically make believing in him easy. He wants us to follow him freely because we love him and trust him, not because we just don't have any choice in the matter!

Preparation

Get together a large suitcase and an assortment of goods to take on a long journey. Have some serious, important items like map, compass (remember faith's a kind of desert journey – the way isn't always clear!), perhaps a first-aid kit and some water purification tablets. Have some fun items, too, such as a pair of woolly bedsocks and a thermal vest, and some ridiculous items (just where are you going to plug in a vacuum cleaner in the desert?), and include some things of sentimental value (genuine or fictitious) that you can't justify on practical grounds but would really hate to leave behind.

Suggested songs

One more step along the world I go
Share in the love of the Lord
Silent, surrendered
Step by step and on and on
We are marching in the light of God

Checklist

At the service, you will need:

• suitcase as above
• flip chart and pens

All-age worship

Opening song

A song praising and celebrating the faithfulness of God

Prayer

Loving God,
we thank you for the promise you give to us,
that you will be our God
and bring about your purpose through us.
Thank you for calling us on a journey of faith.
Forgive us for the times we don't have enough confidence in you,
and help us always to trust you and go forward with you.
Amen.

Word and action

Word: Genesis 12-21
Faith is for people – not camels

(See page 15 for a dramatised version of this story.)

Now, I'll be quite honest – because we camels are *always* honest – when all this started I thought Abram was mad. I mean, he and his wife, Sarai, were perfectly happy living where they were. Maybe Haran was nothing special, but it was OK – and Abram's father was there. Abram and Sarai didn't have any children, but Abram had a nephew, called Lot, and they got on pretty well. Only a human would leave all that to follow a dream – and across the desert, too. They weren't designed for it, of course. In the desert, you need a hump to store water in, and big flat feet to stop you sinking in the sand. In other words, you need a camel – which is why I ended up getting dragged along with them.

Abram reckoned he'd heard this voice, you see – God, he said it was – telling him how he was going to father a great nation and the whole world was going to be blessed through him. Well, I don't know anything about blessings, but at 75 years old I didn't reckon his chances on the fatherhood front.

But, of course, no one who's going on a desert journey ever thinks of consulting an experienced camel – so what did it matter what I thought? Off we went, without a map or a Michelin Guide book between us, and it wasn't long before we had problems. First, Abram got into trouble with the king of Egypt, and only just got himself and Sarai out of there alive. Then Lot – that's his nephew, remember – went off on his own and got into trouble. Finished up in a city called Sodom – which is about as nasty as it sounds – and got himself kidnapped, so Abram had to rescue him.

By this time, even Abram and Sarai were wondering when God was going to keep his promise and start giving them children. I wasn't wondering – I was convinced it was all a load of old orange pips, anyway. But Abram believed it. Apparently God had spoken to him and said, 'Don't worry, Abram – you stick with me and you'll be OK.' As far as I could see, the only good thing this God had done was making them take me along.

Mind you, even Abram wasn't *entirely* sure. I overheard him praying, once. 'Yeah, yeah, I know,' he said, 'but I've still got no children, and neither of us is getting any younger.' But hardly had he finished his prayers before I heard him telling Sarai that God had promised him as many descendants as there were stars in the sky. Now, maybe *you* can count the stars, but *I* can't – I gave up arithmetic when the shekel went metric.

Well, by now Abram was 86 years old, and Sarai wasn't far behind – but he still kept on believing in God's promise. He got a bit impatient at times, mind you – tried to hurry God along and did more harm than good as humans usually seem to – and I did begin to think he'd lost the plot when he said God had promised to turn his family not into just *one* nation but lots of them. This was getting more fantastic all the time.

Next thing I knew, Abram's name changed – to Abraham (and his wife became Sarah). He said God had changed their names when he promised them a lot of land for their descendants to rule over. I'd already heard that bit – I was eavesdropping on Abraham's prayers at the time. He was quiet for a moment, as if listening, and then he burst out laughing. 'Oh, sure!' he said. 'Me, a father at 100 years old – and Sarah a mother when she's 90!' For a minute, I thought he was seeing sense.

Then one day some visitors arrived. Abraham made them welcome, gave them some food and all that. While they were sitting outside, eating, one of them said, 'Where's your wife?'

'In the tent,' Abraham answered. Actually, she was standing at the tent doorway with her ears flapping.

'Well, I'll come back next year,' said the visitor, 'and you can show me your new son.'

Now it was Sarah's turn to laugh. 'What? Me? Old, worn-out, "past-my-best-before-date" me?'

'Why did your wife laugh?' the man asked Abraham.

Sarah was embarrassed. 'Laugh? Me? You must be mistaken, I didn't laugh!' she protested.

'Oh yes, you did,' the man told her. 'You laughed.'

Funny thing, though – soon after that, Sarah started changing. Of course, I recognised the signs – camels are good like that – but it took *them* a long time to catch on. Still, eventually, the great day came and their son was born. Isaac, they called him. Humans – no sense of style. If he'd been a camel he'd have been called Desert Ranger, or Desert Rover, or perhaps Land Ranger or something – but Isaac! Really!

Still, I must admit, Abraham had been right to trust God. I might even try this religion thing, one day.

Action

Open the suitcase and show the congregation the things you've packed in it. Ask them if they can think of any more items you might want to take on a desert journey. Write up their suggestions on a board or flip chart. Have fun with it – encourage them to suggest some frivolous things as well as serious ones: 'What? No copy of Delia Smith?' You might also take the opportunity to bring out the particular talents of some of the congregation: 'Come on, we've got to let Karen take her accordion or what'll we do on the long dark evenings?' Or: 'We'll need a good supply of oranges so Harry can make his wonderful marmalade for us!'

Don't forget about people's recreational needs – a copy of *Pride and Prejudice* might not seem so silly when the novelty of endless sandcastles has worn off.

Then ask how you're going to carry it all. Oh, by the way, you did realise that you were making the journey with nothing more than a few camels? So perhaps you need to think again about that widescreen TV you were going to run off Fred's Range Rover's battery!

It will be very interesting to see what priorities people reveal in the trimming-down process!

Song 2

Offering

This may be introduced as symbolising our commitment to the journey of faith, with its costs as well as its rewards.

Offertory prayer

Accept these gifts, loving God,
as our way of thanking you for your love.
We pray that they may become resources for the journey of faith,
that the world may know your love and your peace.
Amen.

Song 3

Reading

Hebrews 11:8-12 read from a standard Bible. Introduce it with words such as: We read in the New Testament a kind of summary of Abraham's faith story.

Talk (optional)

If you feel it appropriate (and if time permits) point out that, according to Scripture, it was Abraham's faith in God's grace that was important. Even though he made mistakes, his faith meant God could work through him. And as we've seen, faith was about the willingness to take the risk of journeying into the unknown, trusting God to be there and to honour his promise. May that be our faith also.

Notices and family news

Prayers of intercession

Song 4

Closing prayer/benediction

Dramatised reading
Faith is for people – not camels

Narrator Now, I'll be quite honest – when all this started I thought Abram was mad. I mean, he and his wife, Sarai, were perfectly happy living where they were. Maybe Haran was nothing special, but it was OK – and Abram's father was there. Abram and Sarai didn't have any children, but Abram had a nephew, called Lot, and they got on pretty well. Only a human would leave all that to follow a dream – and across the desert, too. They weren't designed for it. In the desert, you need a hump to store water in, and big flat feet to stop you sinking in the sand. In other words, you need a camel – which is why I ended up getting dragged along with them. It all began when Abram heard this voice.

God Hi, Abram. God here. I'm going to use you to start off a whole nation – and the entire world's going to be blessed because of you. Now get packing – you've got a long journey ahead of you.

Abram I say, God, that sounds rather good. [*To Narrator*] Don't you think so, Ermintrude?

Narrator [*Ignoring Abram and talking to audience*] Well, I don't know anything about blessings, but at 75 years old I didn't reckon Abram's chances of being a dad. But if he was going on a desert journey I knew he was going to need an experienced camel around. So off we went, without a map or a Michelin Guide between us, and it wasn't long before we had problems. First, Abram got into trouble with the king of Egypt, and only just got himself and Sarai out of there alive. Then Lot – that's his nephew, remember – went off on his own and got into strife. Finished up in a city called Sodom – which is about as nasty as it sounds – and got himself kidnapped, so Abram had to rescue him. And all that with God still talking in his ear!

God Chill out, Abram – no worries! Stick with me and you'll be OK.

Abram Yes, but I've still got no children, and neither of us is getting any younger. Still, you know best. Hey, Sarai – God says we're going to have as many descendants as there are stars in the sky.

Sarai That's nice, dear. [*Aside*] He's a bit of a dreamer, you know!

Narrator She's right there. Now, maybe *you* can count the stars, but *I* can't – I gave up arithmetic when the shekel went metric. Well, by now Abram was 86 years old, and Sarai wasn't far behind. But he still kept on believing in God's promise.

Abram Sarai, God's told me now that he's going to turn our family into lots of nations – not just one.

Sarai Lovely, dear.

Narrator More fantastic every day! And God was only just getting started.

God Hello, Abram – me again – you know – God. I've been thinking we ought to change your name. Let's make it Abraham from now on – and you can call your wife Sarah. Your descendants

	are going to be kings and queens and rule over the land I'm going to give you.
Abraham	[*Laughing*] Oh, sure! Me, a father at 100 years old – and Sarah a mother when she's 90!
Narrator	For a minute, I thought he was seeing sense. Then one day some visitors arrived. Abraham made them welcome, gave them some food and all that, and sat and chatted with them.
Visitor	Where's your wife?
Abraham	In the tent.
Narrator	Actually, she was standing at the doorway with her ears flapping.
Visitor	Well, I'll come back next year, and you can show me your new son. [*Sarah laughs*] Why did your wife laugh when I said that?
Sarah	[*Embarrassed*] Laugh? Me? You must be mistaken, I didn't laugh!
Visitor	Oh yes, you did. You laughed.
Narrator	Funny thing, though – soon after, Sarah started changing. Of course, *I* recognised the signs – camels are good like that – but it took *them* a long time to catch on. But eventually, the great day came and their son was born. Isaac, they called him. Humans! No sense of style! If he'd been a camel he'd have been called Desert Ranger, or Desert Rover, or perhaps Land Ranger or something – but Isaac! Really! Still, I must admit, Abraham had been right to trust God. I might even try this religion thing, one day.

Moses at the burning bush _____

Preparation page

What's the point?

God challenged Moses, as today he challenges the Church (among others), to become part of his vision. The challenge seemed impossible and Moses' first response was 'I can't do it', but God promised to give him the support and the resources he needed – the trouble was that Moses wouldn't really be sure God had kept his promise until he'd committed himself! Could it be that today God is challenging his Church, and the Church is saying, 'We can't do it'? If so, can we encourage the Church to respond positively to God's call?

Preparation

Make a bush and flames to use in the all-age worship. You can either make a three-dimensional model of a bush from twigs or from wire covered in paper (in which case the 'flames' would eventually be attached using Blu-Tack or loops of thread), or a picture or silhouette on paper, mounted on a large board (in which case pins or Blu-Tack would be used to attach the 'flames'). The 'flames' are simply pieces of irregularly-shaped red and yellow card or paper, large enough to write a short sentence on.

Suggested songs

Be still, for the presence of the Lord
Come, O Lord, inspire us
Lord, the light of your love is shining
Moses, I know you're the man, the Lord said
The voice from the bush

Checklist

At the service, you will need:

- the bush, already in position
- the flame cards to be given out at the door
- some pencils or pens for the congregation
- Blu-Tack or thread to attach the cards to the bush

All-age worship

Opening song

A song praising and celebrating the faithfulness of God

Prayer

Loving God,
we thank you for the challenges you put before us,
calling us to follow you in faith
when we can't be sure of exactly where the journey is taking us,
but trusting you to lead the way.
Please forgive us for the times when our faith is too small
and we make excuses for not following you.
Help us to trust you more,
and to know the joy of journeying with you in faith.
Through Jesus Christ our Lord.
Amen.

Word and action

Word: Exodus 3:1-4:17
Don't ask me!

(See page 21 for a dramatised version of this story.)

This is a story about Moses. He was one of the Israelite people who had been made into slaves by the wicked king of Egypt – or Pharaoh, as they called him. The people were terribly unhappy, but Moses had escaped and was in the desert working as a shepherd. One day, he was out with the sheep when he saw something really strange. A bush was on fire – nothing strange about that, of course, but that wasn't all – although there were flames, the bush didn't actually burn up. 'That's odd,' Moses thought. 'Better take a closer look.'

As he began to walk over, God called out, 'Moses!'

'That's me!'

'Don't come any closer,' God warned him, 'but take your shoes off – this is holy ground you're standing on. I'm God – the God worshipped by your ancestors Abraham, Isaac and Jacob.' That sounded a bit heavy, and Moses was getting more nervous by the minute – so he pulled his cloak over his face.

'I've seen what's going on in Egypt,' God said, 'and I'm not happy. I've seen how miserable my people are, being used as slaves, and now I'm going to do something about it. I'm going to lead them out of Egypt to a new home, and that's where you come in. I'm sending you to Pharaoh to rescue my people from all this misery.'

Moses didn't fancy that idea at all! 'Who? Me? How can I go and tell Pharaoh what to do?'

'You won't be alone,' God assured him. 'I'm going to be right there with you. And before you know it, you'll all be back here worshipping me.'

'But who *are* you?' Moses insisted. 'After all this time in Egypt the people have forgotten you. When I tell them you've sent me, they're going to ask me your name. So what'll I tell them?'

God wasn't falling for that. 'I can be whoever I choose to be,' he answered, 'and I'm greater than any name could express. You go to the Israelite people and tell them that! You can say that I'm the God of your ancestors – the God of Abraham, Isaac and Jacob. That's the only name you'll ever need for me. Now go and tell them all the things I've said to you.'

Things weren't going Moses' way. He didn't want the job at all. 'But what if they don't believe me?' he protested. 'What if they think I'm lying, or crazy or something?'

'What's that you're holding in your hand?' God asked.

'My shepherd's stick,' Moses answered.

'Throw it down on the floor.'

Moses did what God said, and his wooden stick turned into a wriggling snake that frightened Moses so that he started to run away.

'Now pick it up,' God ordered him.

Trembling, Moses reached out and picked up the squirming creature – and straightaway it turned back into a stick. Phew! But God wasn't finished yet. 'Put your hand inside your coat, Moses, and then take it out again,' he said.

When Moses did that, he found his skin had gone white and horrible, but when he did the same thing again, it instantly got better. 'Right,' said God. 'That should convince them, when you do that in Egypt. If not, you can always pour a bit of river water on to the ground and watch me turn it to blood.'

Moses was getting really unhappy, now! 'Look, this sort of thing is all very well,' he said, 'but I'm just not a good speaker – I never have been – it's just not something I do – and that's not going to change just because you've talked to me. You need someone who's good with words – not me!'

'Oh, yes?' God replied. 'And who is it, may I ask, that gives people mouths and tongues, and ears and eyes? I rather thought that was all down to me, actually. Now just go and get on with it – I'll give you all the words you need.'

Moses was desperate. 'No, Lord, please – not me – anyone but me – just go and find someone else. OK?'

God was getting angry. 'Look, you can take your brother Aaron with you – he can talk like it's going out of fashion. So he can do the talking and you can do those things with your stick to show that I mean business.'

Well, there obviously wasn't any point in arguing, so Moses did as God said. And God didn't let him down. Together, they set all the slaves free and led them to the Promised Land. But that's another story.

Action

Point out the bush – we're going to set it on fire with challenges for the church. Divide the congregation into groups and give several red and yellow cards to each group. Ask them to discuss challenges they would put before the church. Examples might be:

- be better represented on community organisations

- provide a more welcoming access for disabled people
- co-operate more with local schools

Give them a few minutes to discuss and write their challenges on their cards. Then ask a representative from each group to come up to the front and tell everybody what is on the cards as each in turn is attached to the bush. You should end up with quite a spectacular 'burning bush' that challenges the church in at least a few realistic ways. Afterwards, the cards can be used in compiling meeting agendas, so the challenges are kept before the church.

Song 2

Offering

This may be introduced as symbolic of our commitment to follow God on the journey of faith on which he is longing to lead us, or our commitment to acknowledge God as our God and try to live in his ways.

Offertory prayer

Loving God,
you challenge us and lead us on a journey
so that we can grow in our faith.
Accept these gifts as a sign of our willingness
to offer what we can and help one another on the way.
Amen.

Song 3

Reading

Mark 1:14-20 read from a standard Bible. Introduce it with words such as: Now we're going to read about Jesus, many centuries later, also calling people on a journey of faith: 'Follow me.'

Talk (optional)

If you feel it appropriate (and if time permits) you could reflect on the gospel's echoes of the Exodus story: the call to follow into the unknown, the need for trust, the fact that Jesus' disciples also found the journey puzzling and threatening at times. Whether you then go on to draw an analogy between the crossing of the Red Sea and Jesus' crossing through death to the other side is up to you – you know your congregation best – but if you do it, keep it light and simple.

Notices and family news

Prayers of intercession

Song 4

Closing prayer/benediction

Dramatised reading
Don't ask me!

In this reading, the part of 'God' could be taken by a number of children reading in turn. As well as involving more children in the story, this would emphasise the point of 'I will be who I will be' – God's nature is too great to be expressed by a single name, or a single personality.

Narrator	This is a story about Moses. He was one of the Israelite people who had been made into slaves by the wicked king of Egypt – or Pharaoh, as they called him. The people were terribly unhappy, but Moses had escaped and was working as a shepherd. One day, he was out with the sheep when he saw something really strange.
Moses	That's odd – that bush is on fire, but it's not being burnt up. Better take a closer look.
God	Moses! Don't come any closer, but take your shoes off – this is holy ground. I'm God – the God worshipped by your ancestors Abraham, Isaac and Jacob. I've seen what's going on in Egypt, and I'm not happy – and now I'm going to do something about it. I'm sending you to Pharaoh to rescue my people.
Moses	Who? Me? How can I go and tell Pharaoh what to do?
God	You won't be alone – I'm going to be right there with you.
Moses	But who *are* you? What's your name?
God	I can be whoever I choose to be, and I'm greater than any name could express. You go to the Israelite people and tell them that!
Moses	But what if they don't believe me? What if they think I'm lying, or crazy or something?'
God	What's that you're holding in your hand?
Moses	My shepherd's stick.
God	Throw it down on the floor.
Narrator	Moses did what God said, and his wooden stick turned into a wriggling snake that frightened Moses so that he started to run away.
God	Now pick it up.
Narrator	Trembling, Moses reached out and picked up the squirming creature by its tail – and straightaway it turned back into a stick. Phew! But God wasn't finished yet.
God	Put your hand inside your coat, Moses, and then take it out again.
Narrator	When Moses did that, he found his skin had gone white and horrible, but when he did the same thing again, it instantly got better.
God	Right. That should convince them, when you do that in Egypt. If not, you can always pour a bit of river water on to the ground and watch me turn it into blood.

Moses Look, this sort of thing is all very well, but I'm just not a good speaker – I never have been – it's just not something I do – and that's not going to change just because you've talked to me. You need someone who's good with words – not me!

God Oh, yes? And who is it, may I ask, that gives people mouths and tongues, and ears and eyes? I rather thought that was all down to me, actually. Now just go and get on with it – I'll give you all the words you need.

Moses No, Lord, please – not me – anyone but me – just go and find someone else. OK?

God You're beginning to make me angry. Look, you can take your brother Aaron with you – he can talk like it's going out of fashion. So he can do the talking and you can do those things with your stick to show that I mean business.

Narrator Well, there obviously wasn't any point in arguing, so Moses did as God said. And God didn't let him down. Together, they set all the slaves free and led them to the Promised Land. But that's another story.

Jesus and Zacchaeus

Preparation page

What's the point?

A better view of life. Jesus' call to salvation involves a change of viewpoint. Zacchaeus saw himself and the rest of the world from a new perspective when he encountered Jesus – and it changed his life. The story indicates that he became other- rather than self-centred after he experienced Jesus' friendship.

Preparation

Make or paint a large tree. Leave the branches fairly bare, and cut some leaves from green paper or card – large enough to write a few words on. Divide the tree into three zones using horizontal lines. Mark the highest zone (from which most can be seen) 'World', the next one 'Community/ Church', and the lowest one (where the closest encounters with people takes place) 'Family/friends'.

Suggested songs

All I once held dear
Jesus had all kinds of friends
Never let Jesus into your heart
Now I know what love is
There was one, there were two (The children's band)
We're going to learn from the poor in the kingdom of heaven
Whether you're one or whether you're two
Zacchaeus was a very little man

Checklist

At the service you will need:

- the tree
- the 'leaf' cards
- some pens or pencils for the congregation
- Blu-Tack or pins

All-age worship

Opening song

A song praising and celebrating the faithfulness of God

Prayer

Loving God,
we thank you for sending Jesus to give us a better view of life.
Thank you for showing that life is richer
if we care for each other.
Forgive us for being selfish,
because we know we all are at times,
and help us to see Jesus as Zacchaeus saw him
and be assured again of your love for us.
Amen.

Word and action

Word: Luke 19:1-10
Zacchaeus gets out of his tree

(See page 27 for a dramatised version of this story.)

Zacchaeus was angry. 'Will somebody shut that guard dog up?' he shouted. 'How's a chap supposed to count his money with that racket going on?'

'Sorry, boss,' said Amos, who was one of his security guards, 'but there's a big crowd outside the gates waiting to see Jesus go by.'

'I don't want excuses,' Zacchaeus yelled. 'Just shut him up. Now, where was I? I'd just got to six million, three hundred and thirty thousand, two hundred and six, or was it six million, three thousand and thirty-two? Oh, bother – now I've got to start all over again.'

Zacchaeus poured himself a glass of wine, and started thinking. 'Jesus mania – whatever next? What's this character got that I haven't, anyway? *He* hasn't got a job – *I'm* the senior tax collector for the whole country. *He* sleeps rough every night – *I've* got a fifty-bedroom mansion with security patrols and guard dogs. (You need those when you're rich.) *He* walks everywhere, or goes scrounging other people's donkeys – *I've* got the very latest chariot from the Bethlehem Mule-cart Works: leather upholstery, sports suspension and a paint job to die for. I mean, I've got the lot. I'm the man – the main man. And still no one loves me. But when a down-at-heel nobody, who talks a load of nonsense about money not being everything, comes to town, suddenly they're excited.'

Somehow, he couldn't concentrate on counting his money any more – he just had to go and see what was so special about this Jesus person. So he called his manservant to get him ready. 'I must look my best,' he said, 'so lay out my most impressive clothes – the ones the king's tailor made for me. And make sure that the label saying "Herod's" is showing on the outside.'

An hour and a half later, Zacchaeus stepped out into the crowded street. No one took any notice of him – they were all straining to get a glimpse of

Jesus. Zacchaeus had to strain a little more than most of them because he was a very small man. Just as he was wondering whether to call his heavies to clear a way through the crowd, he thought, 'Best not to draw attention to yourself when everybody hates you – I'll just climb up this sycamore tree and get a better view.'

He was just in time to see Jesus coming up the road. 'Strange fellow,' he thought. 'His clothes look as though he's slept in them and his beard hasn't been trimmed for weeks – and if I had his manicurist I'd sack her! And yet everyone goes mad for him.'

Then Jesus looked up and saw him. 'Hi, Zacchaeus!'

'Oh, very nice!' thought Zacchaeus. 'Everybody hates me just because I'm a tax man, and now he has to go and draw attention to me in this undignified situation!'

'You'd better come down,' Jesus said. 'I'm having lunch with you today.'

Zacchaeus was amazed. 'Everybody likes you – why d'you want to eat with me? It won't do your popularity any good, you know.' But he came down and took Jesus home with him.

'Come in, Jesus. Mind the burglar trap. Now wait there while I undo these five locks and open the iron door. Sorry about this, but you can't be too careful when you've got wealth to protect. Now come in. GET OUT! No, not you – the guard dog. Sit down. No, not you, Bonzo – I was talking to Jesus. Will someone get this stupid dog out of here?'

Suddenly the house was full of Jesus' friends! Zacchaeus couldn't keep pace. 'Don't put your drink down there, you'll strip the polish! Hey, don't sit on that, it's only for decoration. Put that vase down before you drop it, it's valua– oh, never mind, I can get another.'

They had a great lunch. Jesus' friends might not be Zacchaeus's kind of people but they knew how to have fun – and at least Jesus had some friends! Zacchaeus looked round at the stained tablecloth, the creased cushions, the scratched furniture. 'Oh, why bother!' he heard himself saying. 'I'm going to get shot of all this rubbish. Right, you lot – listen. I'll give half of everything I have to the poor. And if I've fiddled your taxes, I'll pay you back four times over. Now, what else is there? Oh, yes – Simpkins, pop along to the Bethlehem Mule-cart Works and get them to repossess the coupé. Oh, and get the scrap man to collect the iron gate – and have the guard dog retrained as a lap dog. Well, I think that's it – let's start living!'

Zacchaeus had never given anything away before. And he'd never been so happy in his entire life!

Action

Point out that Zacchaeus got a new view on life from his high vantage point – he became other- rather than self-centred – but in order to get the full benefit he had to come down to earth.

Divide the congregation into groups and give each group a few leaves. Point out the three zones in the tree, and ask them to get up good and high in their minds and take a world view. What situations and places do they feel the need to be concerned about? Ask them to do this also at a local church/community level, and then to think of immediate friends and family.

After an appropriate time, ask representatives to come out and read what they have put on their leaves, before sticking or pinning them to the tree. The tree that was once bare has now become rich and green, because the congregation have taken an other-centred viewpoint on the world. Explain that these concerns will later feed into the intercessions. You might like to begin these with a quick résumé of the concerns expressed on the leaves, and then leave appropriate periods of silence for private prayer. The exact way you use this will depend on your knowledge of your congregation and its prayer traditions – the important thing is that the leaves are used prayerfully.

Song 2

Offering

This may be introduced as a sign of our commitment to sharing the new outlook on life that Jesus has given us.

Offertory prayer

Loving God,
we offer you ourselves and our gifts.
Raise us up to see you and your world more clearly,
and then call us back down to earth
to be practical signs of your love within it.
Amen.

Song 3

Reading

1 Corinthians 13 read from a standard Bible. Introduce it with words such as: Jesus' new outlook on life is summed up in the apostle Paul's famous hymn to love. When all other things have perished, love will remain.

Talk (optional)

If you feel it appropriate (and if time permits) you can explain that the word 'salvation' actually means 'wholeness'. In various ways, Jesus' call to salvation is a call to wholeness – and we are more 'whole' when our view of life is fuller. Jesus opens our eyes to the bigger picture, and calls us to 'wholeness'.

Notices and family news

Prayers of intercession

Song 4

Closing prayer/benediction

Dramatised reading
Zacchaeus gets out of his tree

Narrator	Zacchaeus was angry. He was doing what he thought was the most important thing in the world, but he couldn't concentrate.
Zacchaeus	Will somebody shut that guard dog up? How's a chap supposed to count his money with that racket going on?
Amos	Sorry, boss, but there's a big crowd outside waiting to see Jesus go by.
Zacchaeus	I don't want excuses, Amos – just a bit of peace. Now, had I just got to six million, three hundred and thirty thousand, two hundred and six, or was it six million, three thousand and thirty-two? Oh, bother – now I've got to start all over again.
Narrator	Zacchaeus poured himself a glass of wine, and started thinking.
Zacchaeus	Jesus mania – whatever next? What's he got that I haven't, anyway? *He* hasn't got a job – *I'm* the government's senior tax collector. *He* sleeps rough every night – *I've* got a mansion with security patrols and guard dogs. (You need those when you're rich.) *He* walks everywhere, or scrounges other people's donkeys – *I've* got the latest chariot from the Bethlehem Mule-cart Works: leather upholstery, alloy wheels and a paint job to die for. I've got the lot. I'm the main man. And no one loves me. But when a down-at-heel nobody, who talks a load of nonsense about money not being everything, comes to town, suddenly they're excited.
Narrator	Somehow, Zacchaeus couldn't concentrate on counting any more – he just had to go and see what was so special about Jesus.
Zacchaeus	Amos! I must look my best, so lay out my most impressive clothes – the ones the king's tailor made for me. And make sure that the label saying 'Herod's' is showing on the outside.
Narrator	An hour and a half later, Zacchaeus stepped out into the crowded street. No one took any notice of him – they were all straining to get a glimpse of Jesus. Zacchaeus had to strain a little more than most of them because he was a very small man.
Zacchaeus	I could call my heavies to clear a way through the crowd, but it's best not to draw attention to yourself when everybody hates you – I'll just climb up this sycamore tree and get a better view. That's more like it. Strange: his clothes look as though he's slept in them, his beard hasn't been trimmed, and if I had his manicurist I'd sack her! So why's he got more friends than I have?
Jesus	Hi, Zacchaeus!
Zacchaeus	[*Aside*] Oh, very nice! Everybody hates me just because I'm a tax man, and now he has to go and draw attention to me in this undignified situation!

Jesus	You'd better come down – I'm having lunch with you today.
Zacchaeus	[*Amazed*] Everybody likes you – why d'you want to eat with me? It won't do your popularity any good, you know.'
Narrator	But still, Zacchaeus came down and took Jesus home with him.
Zacchaeus	Come in, Jesus. Mind the burglar trap. Now wait there while I undo these five locks and open the iron door. Sorry about this, but you can't be too careful when you've got wealth to protect. Now come in. GET OUT! No, not you – the guard dog. Sit down. No, not you, Bonzo – I was talking to Jesus. Will someone get this stupid dog out of here?
Narrator	Suddenly the house was full of Jesus' friends! Zacchaeus couldn't keep pace.
Zacchaeus	Don't put your drink down there, you'll strip the polish! Hey, don't sit on that, it's only for decoration. Put that vase down before you drop it, it's valua– oh, never mind, I can get another.
Narrator	They had a great lunch. Jesus' friends might not be top people but they knew how to have fun – and at least Jesus had some friends! Zacchaeus looked round at the stained table-cloth, the creased cushions, the scratched furniture.
Zacchaeus	Oh why bother! I'm going to get shot of all this rubbish. Right, you lot – listen. I'll give half of everything I have to the poor. And if I've fiddled your taxes, I'll pay you back four times over. Now, what else is there? Oh, yes – Simpkins, pop along to the Bethlehem Mule-cart Works and get them to repossess the coupé. Well, I think that's it – let's start living!
Narrator	Zacchaeus had never given anything away before. And he'd never been so happy in his entire life!

Great kings

David and Goliath _____

Preparation page

What's the point?

The world is full of apparently powerless people who are oppressed by bullies of one kind or another – whether individuals, governments, big business or whatever. It's important to know that it's worth standing up to these Goliaths.

Preparation

Make a large (ideally, life-size) painting of Goliath, either on a board or several large pieces of paper joined together. You will also need some 'stone' cards for the congregation to write on. Obviously they need to be somewhat bigger than real pebbles to allow for this – about the diameter of a tea cup would be good. Cut them out of buff card and set them aside for the service. Between now and then, find some local issues – for example, the closure of a school or hospital that people value, or the loss of a vital bus service – which affect people but they feel powerless to influence the decisions. If you can't find anything suitable, then a use a fictitious example.

Suggested songs

Goliath was big and Goliath was strong
Jesus is greater than the greatest heroes
Think big: an elephant
When the Spirit of the Lord is within my heart
Whether you're one or whether you're two

Checklist

At the service, you will need:

- the picture of Goliath already on display in the church
- the 'stone' cards
- a supply of pens or pencils for the congregation
- Blu-Tack or pins

All-age worship

Opening song

A song praising and celebrating the faithfulness of God

Prayer

Loving God,
we thank you for knowing us so well,
and loving us as we are.
Forgive us for the times we make snap judgements about people,
based on just what little we know,
and especially when we shut people out because of those judgements.
Help us to love people the way you love them.
Amen.

Word and action

Word: 1 Samuel 17:1-54
The bigger they come . . .

(See page 36 for a dramatised version of this story.)

The battlefield was ready. The armies were facing each other across a valley, the Israelites on one hill and their greatest enemies, the Philistines, on the one opposite. Everyone was nervous, wondering who would start the battle, when out of the Philistine camp came the biggest man anyone had ever seen. Even the mountain looked smaller when he was on it.

'Well, who's going to fight me?'

Goliath's voice echoed horribly from hill to hill and back again, while the Israelite soldiers looked at one another as if to say, 'Don't look at me, mate!' You couldn't blame them. The man was nearly three metres tall – and two would have been quite enough. The armour he was wearing weighed 57 kilograms, which is about as much as a small man or a boy, and that was without counting his helmet. In his hand he had a spear that looked like a rugby post, and the big metal point fixed to the top of it weighed as much as seven bags of sugar. Well, would you have taken him on? Exactly. Neither would I.

He wasn't taking 'No' for an answer, though. 'What are you all doing over there?' he yelled. 'Come on, send one man to fight me. If he kills me, you can have the rest of the army as slaves. But if *I* win – and I rather think I will – then you'll be doing *our* chores for us. Well? Come on – I dare you.'

As Goliath's voice died away, the only sound to be heard in the valley was a strange clattering noise – Israelite knees knocking together with fear. Every soldier was praying, 'Please, God, don't ask me to fight him!' Then they heard a different voice.

'What's his game, then? Who does he think he is? Cheek, I call it, talking to us like that – it's an insult to God, that's what it is! Someone ought to teach him a lesson.' The speaker was young David, the shepherd boy who had come to bring some food to his brothers who were in the army. 'I'll do it,' he went on. 'I'll show that great big pile of mushroom compost that he can't talk to us like that.'

It was probably a good thing the soldiers were so scared, or they might have died laughing. 'You,' one of them said, 'teach *him*? Teach him what? Embroidery?'

In at least one way, David was very like Goliath – *he* wouldn't shut up either. 'I tell you, I can do it – I'm not afraid of him.' Well, eventually they took him to King Saul, and he couldn't shut him up, either. 'I've faced worse than him,' David said. 'I've fought wolves, I've rescued lambs from roaring lions, I've killed hyenas, I've . . .'

'OK, OK,' Saul protested, 'I give in. You'd better borrow my armour, though – I don't think that bit of old sheepskin's going to protect you, unless the smell of it drives Goliath away.'

David tried the armour, but it was no good. 'I'll be quicker on my feet without it. If God can protect me from lions and wolves, I don't need armour against that windbag out there.' And he went. Just like that.

As he crossed the valley, he stopped at the stream, chose five smooth pebbles for ammunition and got his sling at the ready. It was a drill he knew well – all that stuff about wolves and lions wasn't just talk.

Goliath went ballistic when he saw David. 'Is this somebody's idea of a joke,' he bellowed, 'a boy coming to throw stones at me? I'll teach you to mess with Goliath. I'll tear you limb from limb! I'll vivisect you! When I've finished with you, the vultures will think it's Christmas – whatever that is!' With that, Goliath raised his great spear and aimed it at David.

Goliath knew all about fighting. He knew the rules about how to throw a spear, and how to thrust a sword. But there were some things they didn't teach you at the military academy – and the last thing he expected was a stone between the eyes. The *very* last thing he expected . . .

Goliath had never been good at thinking, talking and acting at the same time. So he was fully occupied, shouting his insult, thinking of his next one and aiming his spear, and he simply hadn't got a brain-cell to spare. So he didn't notice David putting a stone into his sling and swinging it round his head. The stone hit Goliath, smack in the middle of his forehead, just as his spear arm was at full stretch. What happened next was a slow-motion action sequence that any cameraman would have been proud of. Perfectly balanced, with his arm locked above his head, Goliath seemed to take a little time for the fact that he was dead to sink in. Then, slowly, his grip relaxed and the massive spear hit the ground just as his knees gave way and his huge body teetered and fell.

Well, things got a bit wild after that, with celebrations and parties – and a few more things I'd rather not tell you about because they were extremely not-very-nice, and quite unnecessary. David went on to become a great king, which only goes to show that size isn't everything.

Action

Ask the congregation what 'Goliath' might represent for them – have your own ideas already lined up in case you need them – and write up one or more of them in big writing around Goliath's head. Now divide the congregation

33

into groups. If there are several issues written up you could designate one for each group – otherwise they can all discuss the same one. The question is what can they do about it? What kind of 'stones' can these apparently powerless people throw at 'Goliath'? Ask them to write the things they think of on their 'stone' cards. As they're discussing things, wander round keeping your ears open for any groups that are struggling, so that you can give them one or two pointers. Examples might be: writing to the newspapers or to their MP; starting a petition; taking part in a demonstration; joining a protest group; raising awareness by an event at church . . .

After an appropriate time, call the groups back to order and ask some people from each group to say what they have written on their stones, and then come and pin or stick them on to the picture of Goliath. It doesn't matter if (as is virtually inevitable) several groups have thought of the same thing – the more there are, the more effective their action might be.

Then look at the beleaguered Goliath and simply observe that we're not as impotent as we may think in the face of the abuse of power.

Song 2

Offering

This may be introduced as a small thing we offer to God that he can take and use for great things in his world.

Offertory prayer

Thank you, Lord, for using whatever we offer,
however small or however imperfect it may be.
So take and use these gifts
so that more people may know of your love.
Through Jesus Christ our Lord.
Amen.

Song 3

Reading

Matthew 21:14-16 read from a standard Bible. Introduce it with words such as: In our Bible reading, Jesus reminds us of the importance of what may seem too small to matter.

Talk (optional)

If you feel it appropriate (and if time permits) stress that we should never underestimate the importance of the 'little people'! These two stories may remind us of how Jesus repeatedly sought to empower those who counted for least or seemed to have least to offer. Maybe there are lessons we can learn there for the way we order church life!

Notices and family news

Prayers of intercession

These could be led entirely by the minister or other adult(s), and/or could include some prayers written by the children themselves – or simply some points that they have raised in discussion.

Song 4

Closing prayer/benediction

Dramatised reading
The bigger they come . . .

Narrator	The battlefield was ready. The armies were facing each other across a valley, the Israelites on one hill and their greatest enemies, the Philistines, opposite. Everyone was wondering who would start, when out of the Philistine camp came an enormous man. Even the mountain looked smaller when he was on it.
Goliath	Well, who's going to fight me?
Narrator	Goliath was nearly three metres tall. His armour weighed 57 kilograms, which is about as much as a small man or a boy, and that was without counting his helmet. He had a spear that looked like a rugby post, and the big metal point fixed to the top of it weighed as much as seven bags of sugar. Well, would you have taken him on? Exactly. Neither would I.
Goliath	What are you all doing over there? Come on, send one man to fight me. If he kills me, you can have the rest of the army as slaves. But if *I* win – and I rather think I will – then you'll be doing *our* chores for us. Well? Come on – I dare you.
Narrator	As Goliath's voice died away, the only sound to be heard in the valley was a strange clattering noise – Israelite knees knocking together with fear! Every soldier was praying, 'Please, God, don't ask me to fight him!' Then they heard a different voice.
David	What's his game, then? Who does he think he is? It's an insult to God. Someone ought to teach him a lesson.
Narrator	The speaker was young David, the shepherd boy who had come to bring some food to his brothers who were in the army.
David	I'll do it. I'll show that great big pile of mushroom compost that he can't talk to us like that.
Soldier	You? Don't be silly!
David	I tell you, I can do it – I'm not afraid of him. I'll teach him!
Soldier	Teach him what? Embroidery?
Narrator	Well, eventually they took David to King Saul, and he couldn't shut him up, either.
David	I've faced worse than him. I've faced hungry wolves, I've rescued lambs from the very jaws of roaring lions, I've killed hyenas, I've –
Saul	OK, OK, I give in. You'd better borrow my armour, though – I don't think that bit of old sheepskin you're wearing is going to protect you, unless the smell of it drives Goliath away.
Narrator	David tried the armour, but it was no good.
David	It'll only slow me down. If God can protect me from lions and wolves, I don't need armour against that windbag out there.
Narrator	As he crossed the valley, he stopped at the stream, chose five smooth pebbles for ammunition and got his sling at the ready. It was a drill he knew well – all that stuff about wolves and lions wasn't just talk. Goliath went ballistic when he saw David.

Goliath   Is this somebody's idea of a joke, a boy coming to throw stones at me? I'll teach you to mess with Goliath. I'll tear you limb from limb! I'll vivisect you! When I've finished with you the vultures will think it's Christmas — whatever that is!

Narrator   With that, Goliath raised his great spear and aimed it at David. Goliath knew all about how to throw a spear, and how to thrust a sword. But he'd never been good at thinking, talking and acting at the same time. So he was fully occupied, shouting his insult, thinking of his next one and aiming his spear, and he simply hadn't got a brain-cell to spare. So he didn't notice David putting a stone into his sling and swinging it round. The stone hit him, smack in the middle of his forehead, just as his spear arm was at full stretch. Goliath seemed to take a little time for the fact that he was dead to sink in. Then, slowly, his grip relaxed and the massive spear hit the ground just as his knees gave way and his huge body teetered and fell. Well, things got a bit wild after that, with celebrations and parties — and a few more things I'd rather not tell you about because they were extremely not-very-nice, and quite unnecessary. David went on to become a great king, which only goes to show that size isn't everything.

Solomon builds the temple

Preparation page

What's the point?

Solomon was wise, and the greatest sign of his wisdom comes in his prayer at the dedication of the temple – God's too great to be contained in our structures. Yet even now, in the twenty-first century, a lot of religious people think they've got God boxed up!

Preparation

In the centre of a large sheet of paper, do a small picture of your own church surrounded by empty space. Over the top, write Solomon's prayer: 'Even the heavens can't contain God.' Have some coloured cards – the more different colours the better – a little smaller than postcards, for the congregation to write on.

Suggested songs

Each of us is a living stone
God's love is deeper
Let us sing your glory, Lord
Our God is so great
Praise God in his holy place
Surely our God is the God of gods
Take me past the outer courts

Checklist

At the service, you will need:

- The church picture, already set up
- The cards for the congregation
- Some pens or pencils for the congregation
- Blu-Tack or pins

All-age worship

Opening song

A song praising and celebrating the faithfulness of God

Prayer

Loving God,
thank you for being the great God you are.
Thank you for being so great
that our minds can't grasp you
and our buildings can't contain you.
Forgive us for the times when we make you seem small,
and help us to be more open to you.
Amen.

Word and action

Word: 2 Chronicles 2:1-6:21
Let's build a temple

(See page 43 for a dramatised version of this story.)

King Solomon had a great idea, and he called his secretary. 'I want you to write a letter to King Hiram of Tyre,' he said.

'Oh, yes,' said the secretary, 'good old King Hiram. I know him well – very good friend of your father's. You know, I remember when . . .'

Solomon interrupted. 'I'm sure you do, but just take the letter, will you. It begins "Dear King Hiram. I've decided to build a temple for God –"'

'Ooh, that's nice,' said the secretary. 'So will God be living there permanently, so he's always right where we want him?'

Solomon sighed. 'You silly secretary-man,' he said. 'Our God's so great even heaven can't contain him, so how could we hold him in a house we built? The best this can ever be will be somewhere for us to worship. But because God's so great, we can't even build that on our own – that's why I need King Hiram's help. Ask him to send us a really good craftsman to do all the wood and metal work and all the curtains and furnishing – we need the very best he's got. Oh, and his woodcutters are far more skilled than ours, so ask him for a supply of timber.'

'That's an awful lot for him to do, Your Majesty,' said the secretary. 'D'you think we should send him some labourers to help?'

Solomon looked surprised. 'You know, that's a really good idea!' he said. 'Tell him that we'll send some workers to work alongside his people. And we'll send him enough food for all of his workers and ours, as well. OK, get that written up neatly – no smudges, now – and send it to King Hiram.'

King Hiram was really pleased. 'King David and I were such good friends,' he said, 'and now Solomon wants my help. Well, it's better than fighting each other all the time, isn't it?' So he sent a letter back to Solomon. 'I think it's great you're king,' he wrote. 'God must really care about his people to give them a wise ruler like you. Of course, I'll be glad to help. I've got a chap here called Huram. He'll work with anything – bronze, silver, gold, stone, wood – and he's handy with a needle and thread, too. Basically, if he can't work with it, you don't want it in your temple anyway.'

So Huram was sent to work with Solomon's labourers and produce all the things they needed for the temple, and King Hiram got his foresters to work cutting the wood that Solomon would need. And, in return, Solomon provided all the food and drink the workers could possibly want.

The temple was amazing – gold everywhere, whole walls covered in it! Even the nails they used were made of gold! Then there was cedarwood panelling, beautiful curtains – it was a breathtaking sight. Part of it was set aside to be the most holy place of all. It had two enormous statues with wings stretched out as if to guard the place. The wings reached right across the room, and the statues were covered in gold. Then Solomon called his secretary again. 'We're going to bring the Covenant Box and put it in the holy of holies.'

'Oh, good!' exclaimed the secretary. 'Then God will be in his house.'

'I've told you before,' Solomon said sternly, 'God's too great for this house – it'll be a place to worship him. And the Covenant Box contains the stones with his law written on them – the ones he gave to Moses in the desert – so we must give that a really special place.'

So they had a big service, with lots of priests and other ministers, and put the special box in the holiest part of the temple. And Solomon said a special prayer.

'Lord God,' he said, 'you're so great even heaven itself isn't big enough for you. So I know this temple can't hold you. But let it be a sign that we love you, and want to be your people, and let it always remind us of your love and your faithfulness to us. Thank you for being such a great and wonderful God. Amen.'

A little bit later, Solomon overheard his secretary talking to the cook and telling him all about the temple. 'Now, whenever you want God,' he said, 'you'll know where to find him.'

Solomon sighed. After all he'd said about how great God is! Some people will just never learn!

Action

Remind the congregation of Solomon's words: 'Even the heavens can't contain God, much less this house'. So we want to know where God's glory is seen *beyond the church* today. Divide the congregation into groups and ask them to discuss this, and write their ideas on the multi-coloured cards. For example, maybe in your locality there are some charities or community groups that show God's love. In the wider world, events must be taking place that show God's power at work. Are there signs of hope between warring nations? Have any news stories caught people's attention? And don't forget the natural world. If people see signs of God's glory in a wonderful sunset or a pretty lily, then that's fine, too. After a short time, call them to order and ask for one or two representatives of each group to come and tell you what they've written (it doesn't matter if two groups actually agree!) and pin or stick the cards around the picture of the church. Soon you should have a really bright and attractive display. Doesn't the whole world look better when we seek God outside our own structures!

Song 2

Offering

This may be introduced with a reminder that all we give to God is really but a small recognition of the infinitely greater gifts he has given to us.

Offertory prayer

Loving God,
we thank you for all your gifts to us.
Accept what we offer here,
and help us to use all you give us wisely,
for the good of your whole creation.
Amen.

Song 3

Reading

Luke 12:22-28 read from a standard Bible. Introduce it with words such as: Jesus recognised Solomon as a great king, and told us to look also for simpler and more immediate signs of God's greatness.

Talk (optional)

If you feel it appropriate (and if time permits) point out that the sheer variety of ways God's glory is shown in the world reflects just how much greater he is than we usually recognise.

Notices and family news

Prayers of intercession

Song 4

Closing prayer/benediction

Dramatised Reading
Let's build a temple

Narrator   King Solomon had a great idea, and he called his secretary.

Solomon   I want you to write a letter to King Hiram of Tyre.

Secretary   Oh, yes, good old King Hiram. I know him well – very good friend of your father's. You know, I remember when . . .

Solomon   I'm sure you do, but just take the letter, will you. It begins 'Dear King Hiram. I've decided to build a temple for God –'

Secretary   Ooh, that's nice. So will God be living there permanently, so he's always right where we want him?

Solomon   [*Sighs*] You silly secretary-man! God's so great even heaven can't contain him, so how could we hold him in a house we built? The best this can ever be will be somewhere for us to worship. But because God's so great, we can't even build that on our own – that's why I need King Hiram's help. Ask him to send us a really good craftsman to do all the wood and metal work and all the curtains and furnishing – we need the very best he's got. Oh, and his woodcutters are far more skilled than ours, so ask him for a supply of timber.

Secretary   That's an awful lot for him to do, Your Majesty. D'you think we should send him some labourers to help?

Solomon   [*Surprised*] You know, that's a really good idea! Tell him that we'll send some workers to work alongside his people. And we'll send him enough food for all of his workers and ours, as well. OK, get that written up neatly – no smudges, now – and send it to King Hiram.

Narrator   King Hiram was really pleased.

Hiram   King David and I were such good friends, and now Solomon wants my help. Well, it's better than fighting each other all the time, isn't it? Dan, take a letter. 'To King Solomon, Jerusalem: I think it's great you're king. God must really care about his people to give them a wise ruler like you. Of course, I'll be glad to help. I've got a chap here called Huram. He'll work with anything – bronze, silver, gold, stone, wood – and he's handy with a needle and thread, too. Basically, if he can't work with it, you don't want it in your temple anyway.'

Narrator   So Huram was sent to work with Solomon's labourers and produce all the things they needed for the temple, and King Hiram got his foresters to work cutting the wood that Solomon would need. And, in return, Solomon provided all the food and drink the workers could possibly want. The temple was amazing – gold everywhere – whole walls covered in it! Even the nails they used were made of gold! Then there was cedarwood panelling, beautiful curtains – it was a breathtaking sight. Part of it was set aside to be the most holy place of all. It had two enormous statues with wings stretched out as if to guard the place. The wings reached right across the room, and the statues were covered in gold. Then Solomon called his secretary again.

Solomon   We're going to bring the Covenant Box and put it in the holy of holies.

Secretary   Oh, good! Then God will be in his house.

Solomon   [*Sternly*] I've told you before, God's too great for this house – it'll be a place to worship him. And the Covenant Box contains the stones with his law written on them – the ones he gave to Moses in the desert – so we must give that a really special place.

Narrator   So they had a big service, with lots of priests and other ministers, and put the special box in the holiest part of the temple. And Solomon said a special prayer.

Solomon   Lord God, you're so great even heaven itself isn't big enough for you. So I know this temple can't hold you. But let it be a sign that we love you, and want to be your people, and let it always remind us of your love and your faithfulness to us. Thank you for being such a great and wonderful God. Amen.

Narrator   A little bit later, Solomon overheard his secretary talking to the cook and telling him all about the temple.

Secretary   Now, whenever you want God, you'll know where to find him.

Narrator   Solomon sighed. After all he'd said about how great God is! Some people will just never learn!

Jesus: A king on a borrowed donkey

Preparation page

What's the point?

Jesus' entry into Jerusalem was seen as a challenge to the authorities. Perhaps, though, we could also see it as a challenge to the people's idea of what a king should be.

Preparation

Make a display of different types of transport. The simplest way would be to use pictures cut from magazines, and pasted on to a large sheet of paper. Try and get a varied selection – helicopter, limousine, family hatchback, bicycle, milk-float, delivery van – and include an obviously royal coach of some kind. Then think of the kinds of people who would use these different forms of transport, and write them on cards: rock singer, king/queen, company director, newspaper deliverer, and so on.

Suggested songs

I will wave my hands
Jesus rode a donkey into town
Sing hosanna
There was one, there were two (The children's band)
We have a king who rides a donkey

Checklist

At the service, you will need:

- the display already in place
- the cards
- Blu-Tack or pins

All-age worship

Opening song

A song praising and celebrating the faithfulness of God

Prayer

Loving God, we come here to worship you.
Thank you for showing us that your power is different
from the power worldly rulers have.
Forgive us when we think and talk as though you are like them,
and help us to show in our lives that we serve you,
and it makes a difference.
Amen.

Word and action

Action

Call attention to the display of different forms of transport, produce the cards and ask the congregation to decide where to put each one. The rock star might go beside a picture of a helicopter, or a very 'flash' sports car, for example. After the cards have been placed, have the story read in either narrative or dramatised form. What sort of king comes into town on a donkey's back? A very different kind of king from the kind that most of us are familiar with!

People's transport may be seen as making a statement about them – and Jesus' choice of a humble donkey made a statement about his kind of kingship.

Word: Luke 19:28-40
He's king in a different way

(See page 49 for a dramatised version of this story.)

Jesus was on his way to Jerusalem – and his friends were getting excited.

'This is it,' said John to his brother, James. 'He's going to take over – show them he's in charge.'

'Well, about time too,' said James. 'We've been waiting long enough – it's time for that King Herod to find out who the real king is around here.'

'King of people's hearts is what I want to be,' Jesus reminded them, 'not the kind that bosses everyone about.' But they were so excited about the 'king' bit they never heard any of the rest.

'If you really want to do something important,' said Jesus, 'you can go and get me something to ride on when we get to Jerusalem.'

'A horse!' shouted John, gleefully. 'A big, white horse with its own armour and a proper saddle with one of those little things to put your spear in.'

'Well, a donkey actually,' Jesus answered. 'In fact, a young donkey that no one's ever ridden before.'

James was surprised. 'I know we're poor,' he said, 'but this is your one big chance. You've got to make an impression.'

'Oh, I'm going to make an impression, all right,' Jesus assured him, 'but if you think I'm going into Jerusalem done up like some kind of warlord, you've got me all wrong. Just go and get the colt for me. You'll find it just inside the village. If anyone asks you why you're taking it, just say that I need it.'

So off went James and John. 'I know what it is!' exclaimed James. 'He's playing it clever – going to sneak up on them and then strike when they're not ready.'

As he spoke, they arrived on the outskirts of Bethany where Jesus was well known. They found the colt and untied it – the owner stopped objecting when they told him who wanted it – and they brought it to Jesus.

'Couldn't you have found something better than this!' scoffed Peter. 'I'm surprised it's not wearing a nappy!'

'It hasn't even got a saddle!' exclaimed Bart. 'Here, Jesus – you'd better sit on my coat.'

Some of the other disciples also put their coats on the donkey's back, and Jesus sat down. As they set out for Jerusalem there was a feeling of excitement among the disciples. They were sure this must be the big moment when God was going to give them the power to rule over everybody else.

As they approached Jerusalem, people came running to spread their coats on the road – that was their way of welcoming a great leader. On and on they travelled, with the noise growing louder all the time. People started shouting to one another about the great things they knew Jesus had done.

'He healed my daughter,' said one.

'He helped me not to feel guilty all the time,' said another.

'He cured me of a horrible disease,' a third chipped in.

'I know,' came the reply. 'If he hadn't I wouldn't be standing anywhere near to you!'

There were some people in the crowd, though, who weren't enjoying it one little bit.

Simon, the Pharisee, turned to his friend Nick and said, 'If this racket goes on, the Governor will think there's a revolution starting – and he'll blame us for it. We've got to find a way to shut this crowd up.'

'I agree,' Nick answered, 'but what can we do about it? No one's going to listen to us – they're all far too excited for that.'

'I just don't get it,' Simon grumbled. 'We look the part – all the right clothes and everything – and we're supposed to be the respected leaders around here – and no one listens to us. But give them a scruffy carpenter who hasn't combed his hair, and they're all over him.'

'Well, you must admit, he's a nice guy,' Nick pointed out, 'and he really does love people.'

'I'm getting worried about you,' Simon said, threateningly. 'You wouldn't be falling for his patter as well, would you? Anyway, love's got nothing to do with it. Religion's about good behaviour – not love.' With that, Simon pushed through the crowd to get to Jesus. 'Here,' he shouted, 'are you going to shut these people up before some trouble starts?'

Jesus smiled at Simon. 'Shut them up?' he said. 'There's so much happiness around today that if they didn't shout the stones probably would!'

Later, as James and John returned the donkey to its owner, they were puzzled. 'What was all that about?' James wondered aloud. 'All that fuss, and he didn't make himself king. Nothing's changed.'

'Oh, I don't know,' John replied. 'I know he doesn't have a throne or a crown or anything, but perhaps he's our king in a different way.'

Song 2

Offering

This may be introduced as a token of our recognition of Jesus' kingship in our own lives, as we bring our offerings to him.

Offertory prayer

Lord Jesus,
we offer you ourselves and our gifts.
Help us to use them well,
that the world may come to recognise your gentle rule of love.
Amen.

Song 3

Reading

1 Corinthians 1:22-31 read from a standard Bible. Introduce it with words such as: We are reminded that God not only values what seems small or silly to us, but can use it to do great things.

Talk (optional)

If you feel it appropriate (and if time permits) simply point out that Jesus accomplished much more in his 'weakness' and 'foolishness' than any of his antagonists managed in their 'strength'. We can see the reality of this in our ordinary relationships where we have to make ourselves vulnerable, refrain from the use of power and force, in order to enable real love to grow. And the story of Jesus tells us that that's God's way – and that it works!

Notices and family news

Prayers of intercession

Song 4

Closing prayer/benediction

Dramatised reading
He's king in a different way

Narrator	Jesus was on his way to Jerusalem – and his friends James and John were getting excited.
John	This is it, James. He's going to take over.
James	Well, about time too. We've been waiting long enough – it's time for that King Herod to find out who the real king is around here.
Narrator	Jesus was sad to hear them talking like that.
Jesus	King of people's hearts is what I want to be – not the kind that bosses everyone about. If you really want to do something important, go and get me something to ride on.
John	[Gleefully] A horse! A big, white horse with its own armour and a proper saddle with one of those little things to put your spear in.
Jesus	Well, a donkey actually. A young one no one's ever ridden before.
James	I know we're poor, but this is your chance to make an impression.
Jesus	Oh, I'm going to make an impression all right, James, but not by going into Jerusalem done up like some kind of warlord. Go and get the colt. It's just inside the village. If anyone asks, just say I need it.
Narrator	So off they went. James thought he knew what Jesus was up to.
James	I know what it is! He's playing it clever – going to sneak up on them and then strike when they're not ready.
Narrator	As James spoke, they arrived on the outskirts of Bethany where Jesus was well known. They found the colt and untied it – the owner stopped objecting when they told him who wanted it – and they brought it to Jesus. Peter wasn't impressed at all.
Peter	[Scoffing] Couldn't you have found something better than this? Look, Bart – I'm surprised it's not wearing a nappy!
Bart	It hasn't even got a saddle! Here, Jesus – sit on my coat.
Narrator	Some of the other disciples also put their coats on the donkey's back, and Jesus sat down. As they set out for Jerusalem there was a feeling of excitement. The disciples were sure this must be the big moment when God was going to give them the power to rule over everybody else. As they approached Jerusalem, people came running to spread their coats on the road – that was their way of welcoming a great leader. On and on they travelled, with the noise growing

louder all the time. People started shouting to one another about the great things they knew Jesus had done.

Bystander 1	He healed my daughter.
Bystander 2	He helped me not to feel guilty all the time.
Bystander 3	He cured me of a horrible disease.
Narrator	There were some people in the crowd, though, who weren't enjoying it one little bit. Simon, the Pharisee, and his friend Nick.
Simon	If this racket goes on, the Governor will think there's a revolution starting – and he'll blame us for it. We've got to find a way to shut this crowd up.
Nick	I agree, but what can we do about it? No one's going to listen to us – they're all far too excited for that.
Simon	I just don't get it. We look the part – all the right clothes and everything – and we're supposed to be the respected leaders around here – and no one listens to us. But give them a scruffy carpenter who hasn't combed his hair, and they're all over him.
Nick	Well, you must admit, he's a nice guy, and he really loves people.
Simon	[*Threateningly*] I'm getting worried about you. You wouldn't be falling for his patter as well, would you? Anyway, love's got nothing to do with it. Religion's about good behaviour – not love.
Narrator	With that, Simon pushed through the crowd to get to Jesus.
Simon	Are you going to shut these people up before trouble starts?
Jesus	[*Smiling*] Shut them up? There's so much happiness around today that if they didn't shout the stones probably would!
Narrator	Later, as James and John returned the donkey to its owner, they were puzzled.
James	What was all that about? All that fuss, and he didn't make himself king. Nothing's changed.
John	Oh, I don't know . . . I know he doesn't have a throne or a crown or anything, but perhaps he's our king in a different way.

God of new beginnings

Creation: In the beginning, God . . . _____

Preparation page

What's the point?

God's wonderful, loving creativity. In this story he gives creation space to grow; he works by invitation and response. What a wonderful model for our creative relationships with one another!

Preparation

Create a barren landscape, either by using a box of sand or by securing some pieces of oasis together. If you use sand, it will need to be firmly packed to allow things stuck into it to stand upright. Test it with a drinking straw. Now draw rough outlines (no detail – the cards need to be blank for writing on) of flower heads. Make them about 10-12cm across, to allow space for a few words to be written on them. Use sticky tape to fix the heads to drinking-straw 'stalks'. As an added feature, you might like to prepare a sign to go above the landscape with the name of your town/village/district on it.

Suggested songs

Let love be real*
Let us sing your glory, Lord
O Lord, my God
Our God is so great
Send forth your Spirit, Lord
There are hundreds of sparrows

Checklist

At the service, you will need:

- the landscape
- the card flowers

* The modified text in *21st Century Hymnal* is more appropriate than that in *The Children's Hymnbook* which originated as a love-song in a musical.

All-age worship

Opening Song

A song praising and celebrating the faithfulness of God

Prayer

Great Creator God,
we thank you for all the beauty and wonder of your creation.
Thank you for giving us the privilege of working with you
to help creation grow and flourish.
Forgive us when we exploit for our own selfish gain
the wonderful things you gave us to care for,
and help us to live and work more closely with you.
Amen.

Word and action

Word: Genesis 1:1-2:3
Let's get creative

(See page 57 for a dramatised version of this story.)

In the beginning, God decided to create the universe. To be honest, it wasn't very pretty at first – in fact, it was pretty untidy. And it was dark – really, really dark.

So God started by dealing with that. 'Let there be light!' he said. And there was. And it was good. And God liked it. So God separated it from the darkness. 'I'll call the light "day" and the darkness "night",' he thought. So of course the first day had gone.

Now, light's a wonderful thing – but as you know, it shows up an untidy bedroom something terrible. 'Man, what a mess!' said God. 'Better tidy up and make a bit of space to work. I'll make a start with all this water. Water's nice in its place – but this isn't in the place at all. What we need is a big dome – I can keep some of the water above it and some underneath, and that'll make a nice bit of sky.' And it happened, just as he said. And that took care of the second day.

'Now, let's see,' God mused. 'Let's have all the water under the dome pulled together so that some land can appear. That's terrific. So I'll call the land earth and the water sea. Wonderful!'

And it was. So, with things tidied up a bit, God had some nice spaces he could work in. So he spoke to the earth. Yes, I know it sounds silly, but if you're God, you can do that sort of thing – and it works. 'Let's see what you can produce,' he said. 'Lots of plants with seeds in them – and some trees, as well – lovely fruit trees with seeds in the fruit so they'll produce even more.'

In a flash, the dull brown earth sprouted millions of colours: lots of green stuff – can you think of any . . .? And trees with red berries . . . And some yellow flowers . . . And some fruit trees . . . Well, all ways round it looked pretty amazing. 'That's great!' said God. But by then it was evening, and then came the morning: the third day had passed.

'Well, well, well,' said God. 'Morning already! Time to be at it. Let's put some nice lights in the sky – a bright sun for the day, and a gentle night light as well – a moon's what we need, I think, and some pretty stars. Now, they could be really useful – they could help keep track of the seasons so we don't get rhododendrons blooming in the winter and catching cold. There, now, although I say it myself, it's shaping up really well!' So the evening came, and then the morning – the fourth day.

'Right,' said God. 'Time to have a chat with the sea now. Come on, you oceans – I want animals this time. Lots of fish, great sea monsters, tiny little crabs – you name it, I want it.' [*So how about naming a few?*] 'Oh,' he went on, 'and let's have some birds flying in the sky, too . . . Oh yes! Most satisfactory. Well, would you believe it? – another day gone. What's that – I make it five.'

'Hello, hello, hello,' said God. 'Morning already? Well, time to talk to the earth again – it worked a treat last time. Now, you can produce lots of animals: everything from cows to creepy crawlies. Wonderful! Hey, I just *love* those horses in pyjamas! Right – what next? Well, what else could there be? Time for the real work of art. No, thank you, earth – I'm taking complete charge of this myself. This is special. I'll make people. They'll be like me, so they can think and love and be really creative – and they'll help the earth and all the animals and other creatures to do well – I'll put them in charge of it and we'll work together. Yes, that sounds terrific.'

So God created people. He made them just like himself. He made both men and women, and he blessed them. 'Everything's ready,' he said. 'I've prepared a wonderful earth for you. So go and have lots of children, and spread out over the whole earth to look after it. Care for the animals as well, and for the fish and the birds – oh, and don't forget the flowers and trees. It's all your responsibility now. There's lots of food for you and for the animals – oh, my word, I'm happy!'

Did God say 'happy'? Ecstatic more like it. But time flies when you're enjoying yourself: evening came, and then morning, and the sixth day had gone.

'Just one more thing,' God said. 'I've got to invent rest – a day set aside for love, friendship, worship – anything but work. Work six, rest one; work six, rest one; work six . . . that's it – get some rhythm going. Now that's *really* good.'

Action

Have the story read in either narrative or dramatised form, and then draw attention to the barren landscape. If you've done the sign, you can say, 'Is this what our area's really like?' No doubt there are some aspects that are like that, but some that are not. Divide the congregation into groups and give out the card flowers. Ask them to discuss where the opportunities are for God's creativity to show in your area. Is there a thriving youth club that gives young people a healthy social outlet? Is there, perhaps, a Toc H or Round Table that provides a sign of God's goodness in the area, or a dramatic society that brings people of different ages and circumstances together? Are you particularly well blessed with your local medical or dental centre, or is there a nice park for people to enjoy? What about the gifts of people in the congregation? Do you have talented musicians, craftworkers, artists? Is the church providing, or could it provide important services to the community? What about the pastoral care that goes on in the church? These are just examples of ideas that you might have in mind in order to prompt any groups that are struggling. Ask them to write the things they think of on the cards. If – or, rather, when – more than one group think of the same things, that doesn't matter. Having more flowers with that item on will show its enhanced value in the community.

After a suitable time, call the groups together and ask them to tell the rest of the congregation what they have written on their flowers as they come forward and plant the flowers in the oasis or sand to make the barren landscape blossom with signs of God's creativity. Now *that's* what God calls us all to be part of – and it's a pretty exciting thing to be involved in, isn't it?

Song 2

Offering

This may be introduced as our offering of ourselves, our talents, our faith, for God to use in making creation whole.

Offertory prayer

Loving God,
we thank you for all the wonder of your creation,
but most of all for the privilege you give us
of being partners with you in the creative process.
Accept what we offer of ourselves and our possessions,
that creation may once again be whole,
and we may know the joy of perfect relationship with you.
Amen.

Song 3

Reading

Matthew 6:25-30 read from a standard Bible. Introduce it with words such as: Jesus reminds us of God's continual care for every part of his creation.

Talk (optional)

If you feel it appropriate (and if time permits) point out that, for all that's wrong with the world, goodness and beauty stubbornly refuse to be extinguished. One possible response when people say, 'How can you believe in a good God when the world's as it is?' might be to point out the very fact that goodness, despite its apparent frailty, survives against such apparently insuperable odds.

Notices and family news

Prayers of intercession

Song 4

Closing prayer/benediction

Dramatised reading
Let's get creative

As there is only one 'character' in this story, it's recommended that the narrator's part be divided between a number of children. You needn't limit it to three.

Narrator 1	In the beginning, God created the universe. At first, it was pretty untidy. And it was dark – really dark. So God spoke.
God	Let there be light!
Narrator 2	And there was.
Narrator 3	And it was good.
Narrator 1	And God liked it. So he separated it from the darkness.
God	I'll call the light 'day' and the darkness 'night'.
Narrator 2	So of course the first day had gone.
Narrator 3	Now, light's a wonderful thing – but as you know, it shows up an untidy bedroom something terrible – and God noticed.
God	Man, what a mess! Better tidy up and make a bit of space to work. I'll start with all this water. We need a big dome for a sky – I can keep some of the water above it and some underneath.
Narrator 1	And it happened, just as he said. And that was the second day.
God	Now, let's see. Let's bring all the water under the dome together so that some land can appear. That's terrific. So I'll call the land earth and the water sea. Wonderful!
Narrator 2	So, having made a tidy space to work, God spoke to the earth.
Narrator 1	What?
Narrator 2	I know, but if you're God, you can do that sort of thing
God	Let's see what you can produce. Lots of plants with seeds in them – and some lovely fruit trees with seeds in the fruit.
Narrator 3	In a flash, the dull brown earth sprouted millions of colours. Well, all ways round it looked pretty amazing. God loved it!
Narrator 2	But by then it was evening, and then came the morning.
Narrator 3	The third day had passed.
God	Let's put some nice lights in the sky – a bright sun for the day, and a gentle night light – a moon, and some pretty stars. Now, they could be really useful – they could help keep track of the seasons so we don't get rhododendrons blooming in the winter and catching cold. There, now, it's shaping up really well!
Narrator 1	So the evening came, and then the morning – the fourth day.
God	Right – come on, you oceans – give me some animals. Lots of fish, great sea monsters*. Oh, and let's have some birds in the sky, too . . . Marvellous!

* Let the children suggest names here.

Narrator 2 Night came, and then morning. That was the fifth day.

God Now, earth – you can produce lots of animals. Wonderful! Hey, I just *love* those horses in pyjamas! Right – time for the real work of art – and I'm taking charge of this myself. I'll make people. They'll be like me, so they can think and love and be creative – and they'll help creation to do well – I'll put them in charge of it and we'll work together. Yes, that sounds terrific.

Narrator 3 So God created people. He made them just like himself. He made both men and women, and he blessed them.

God Everything's ready – I've prepared a wonderful earth for you. So go and have lots of children, and spread out over the whole earth to look after it. It's all your responsibility now. There's lots of food for you and for the animals – oh, my word, I'm happy!

Narrator 1 Did God say 'happy'? Ecstatic more like it. But time flies when you're enjoying yourself.

Narrator 2 Evening came, and then morning, and the sixth day had gone.

God Day seven. One thing left to make: rest – a day set aside for love, friendship, worship – anything but work. Work six, rest one; work six, rest one; work six . . . that's it – get some rhythm going. Now that's *really* good.

Jesus: In the new beginning, God . . . _____

Preparation page

What's the point?

A new vision of God. There are none so blind as those who will not see! This man, although physically blind, could 'see' things other people couldn't – especially the spiritually-blind Pharisees. Their idea of religion as a matter of keeping rules had hardened their hearts and blinded their insight, so when the God of love stood right before their eyes they couldn't recognise him. All too often our religion can get like that – but Jesus can give us a new vision of a God who loves us and longs for us to have *real* life!

Preparation

Draw a large picture of a donkey with no tail. Then cut it out and paste it on to another piece of paper or card. That should leave a definable ridge around the outline which is not obvious from a distance. Draw a tail on a separate piece of card, or make one from string and attach a drawing pin to the 'body' end.

Suggested songs

Be still, for the presence of the Lord
Lord, the light of your love is shining
The Spirit lives to set us free (Walk in the light)
This little light of mine

Checklist

At the service, you will need:

- the donkey picture
- the tail – complete with pins or Blu-Tack

All-age worship

Opening song

A song praising and celebrating the faithfulness of God

Prayer

Loving God,
thank you for the vision you put in front of us as your people.
We pray that as we worship you,
you will open our eyes to recognise you and your challenge.
Please forgive us for the times we refuse to see
because we're afraid of that challenge,
and help us to go from here filled with a sense of your love
and longing to be caught up in your work.
Amen.

Word and action

Action

Invite the congregation to play a game – it's fun, but it makes a serious point. Put up the donkey picture, and invite some people to have a go at pinning the tail on the donkey. Blindfold each volunteer before they get too close (you don't want them seeing your secret!) and guide them forward to stand in front of the donkey. Then give them the tail and the pin, and let them have a go. Some may notice that they can feel the outline – others may not. If nobody notices, you can secretly whisper to one or two of them what the secret is, and then they should be able to get reasonably close.

Finally, reveal the trick to the congregation. You'll probably get a few groans and calls of 'cheat!' but you can point out that what was not obvious to the congregation, who thought they could see, was much more obvious to the 'blind' people, who got close enough to use another of their senses. But they had to get close to do it, and be open to other senses than sight. Now they're going to hear a story about a man who was blind, but who was able to 'see' much more than the sighted people around him.

Word: John 9:1-41
Can't see the love for the rules

(See page 63 for a dramatised version of this story.)

Seth was having just another ordinary day – until Jesus walked by, and that changed his life for ever. The first he knew of it was when he heard one of Jesus' friends ask a question – Seth couldn't see Jesus because he was blind, but his hearing was really sharp.

'OK, then,' Seth heard one of them say. 'Whose sin made this man blind – was it something he did wrong, or something his parents did?'

Seth could have been very angry, but he was used to that kind of silliness by now. He didn't know who these people were, but perhaps if he ignored them they'd go and irritate someone else. Then he heard another voice, answering. And it made him pay attention.

'Oh, grow up!' said the voice. 'You can't blame either him or his parents for this – but as he's blind it's a chance to show God's love.'

Seth waited for the usual pat on the head and quick blessing he sometimes got. He found it seriously annoying – people thought they were being nice by treating him like a pet poodle, and he knew they meant well but wished they'd do something really helpful.

Suddenly, Seth felt something warm and sticky being put on his eyes. Jesus had made some mud from the sand on the ground.

Seth wasn't impressed. 'Hey, what's the idea!'

'Don't worry,' came the kind voice. 'Go and wash that off in the pool.'

'You bet I will – what a liberty!' Seth went off angrily to the pool they called Siloam. He quickly scooped up the water in his hands and washed his eyes. 'Eh? What's that?' Suddenly he could see a bright light. Then he began to make out shapes. He could see! For the first time ever! He started shouting for joy, and people began to notice. Well, they would, wouldn't they?

'Oh, so you can see, can you? So why were you begging for money before?' someone demanded.

'Well, I *couldn't* see then,' Seth answered. 'It's a miracle.'

'Oh, very convenient,' sneered Simon, the Pharisee. 'When it suited you to be a beggar you were blind, and now for some reason you've decided to admit you can see.'

'It's not like that,' Seth protested. 'I *was* blind – but this man put something on my eyes, and now I can see.'

Simon pricked up his ears. 'I bet "someone" was that Jesus,' he thought. He turned to Seth. 'Well, whoever he was, he's a bad man,' he said. 'He was working on the official day of rest – and that's against God's law.'

Suddenly, the people around were arguing among themselves, and no one could agree whether Jesus was a great man of God or a criminal! So Simon and the other Pharisees turned to Seth. 'Who do *you* think he is – after all, it was your eyes he opened?'

Seth couldn't believe his ears. 'He's a great prophet, of course,' he answered. 'It's obvious, isn't it?'

Simon and his friends weren't expecting that. Seth knew jolly well what they'd wanted him to say – that Jesus was a bad man. So they called Seth's parents. 'Your son hasn't really always been blind, has he?' they said. 'Own up, now – it was all a big con, wasn't it?'

'Oh, no,' said Seth's dad, 'he was blind all right – we're really thrilled about this.'

'Oh, you are, are you? So who do *you* think Jesus is?' Simon challenged him.

Seth's dad wasn't going to get caught like that. He knew that anyone who said good things about Jesus was banned from going to worship ever again. 'Seth's a big boy now,' he said. 'Ask him.' And he took his wife's arm and hurried quickly away.

Simon turned back to Seth. 'Come on,' he said, 'admit it – Jesus is a crook, isn't he?'

Seth looked patient. 'That's not for me to say,' he said. 'But I do know that once I was blind, and now I can see. And if it comes to that, I can see the blindingly obvious when it's right in front of me, which is more than you can, and you reckon you're not blind! It's all those precious rule books – you can't see past them!'

Simon was furious. 'Oh, you're a bad lot,' he shouted angrily. 'You always have been. You were born bad, and bad is what you'll always be. Never darken the door of my synagogue again.'

'Suits me,' Seth retorted. 'My eyes have been opened to see what's good. I don't want to end up blind to it again, like you. Now, where's this Jesus fellow got to – I think it's time we had a word.'

Song 2

Offering

This may be introduced as symbolising our contribution to the new beginning God is longing to make in our lives and communities.

Offertory prayer

Loving God,
we thank you for always putting fresh challenges before your people,
and new hope in the world.
Use these gifts of ourselves and our possessions
to enable a new beginning in faith for us and for others.
Amen.

Song 3

Reading

Isaiah 43:18-21 read from a standard Bible. Introduce it with words such as: Through the prophet Isaiah, God calls us to be on the alert, looking for the new things he's doing – the new opportunities he's putting before the churches and the world, today.

Talk (optional)

If you feel it appropriate (and if time permits) you can point out that Jesus' new beginning challenged the old, accepted religious ideas and practices. That didn't mean he didn't value his traditions, but he never allowed the 'We've always done it this way' brigade to get in the way of his healing and saving work.

Notices and family news

Prayers of intercession

Song 4

Closing prayer/benediction

Dramatised reading
Can't see the love for the rules

Narrator	Seth was having just another ordinary day – until Jesus walked by, and that changed his life for ever. The first he knew of it was when he heard one of Jesus' friends ask a question.
Disciple	OK, then, whose sin made this man blind – was it something he did wrong, or something his parents did?
Narrator	Seth could have been very angry, but he was used to that kind of silliness by now. He didn't know who these people were, but perhaps if he ignored them they'd go and irritate someone else. Then he heard another voice, and it made him pay attention.
Jesus	Oh, grow up! You can't blame either him or his parents for this – but as he's blind it's a chance to show God's love.
Narrator	Seth waited for the usual pat on the head and quick blessing he sometimes got. He found it really annoying – people thought they were being nice by treating him like a pet poodle. But instead, he felt something warm and sticky being put on his eyes. Jesus had made some mud from the sand on the ground.
Seth	Hey, what's the idea!
Jesus	Don't worry. Go and wash that off in the pool.
Seth	[*Angrily*] You bet I will – what a liberty!
Narrator	Seth went off angrily to the pool they called Siloam. He quickly scooped up the water in his hands and washed his eyes.
Seth	Eh? What's that?
Narrator	He could see a bright light. Then he began to make out shapes. He could see! For the first time ever! He started shouting for joy, and people began to notice. Well, they would, wouldn't they.
Bystander	Oh, so you can see, can you? So why were you begging for money before?
Seth	Well, I *couldn't'* see then. It's a miracle.
Simon	Oh, very convenient! When it suited you, you were blind, and now for some reason you've decided to admit you can see.
Seth	Trust a Pharisee to say something like that! It's simple – I *was* blind, but someone put something on my eyes, and now I can see.
Simon	[*Aside*] I bet 'someone' was that Jesus. [*To Seth*] Well, whoever he was, he's a bad man. He was working on the official day of rest – and that's against God's law.
Narrator	Suddenly, the people around were arguing among themselves, and no one could agree whether Jesus was a great man of God or a criminal! So Simon and the other Pharisees turned to Seth.
Simon	Who do *you* think he is – after all, it was your eyes he opened?

Seth	He's a great prophet, of course. It's obvious, isn't it?
Narrator	Simon and his friends weren't expecting that. Seth knew jolly well what they'd wanted him to say – that Jesus was a bad man – so they called Seth's parents.
Simon	Your son hasn't really always been blind, has he? Own up, now – it was all a big con, wasn't it?
Seth's dad	Oh, no, he was blind all right – we're really thrilled about this.
Simon	Oh, you are, are you? So who do *you* think Jesus is?
Seth's dad	[*Aside*] I'm not going to get caught like that. I know that anyone who says good things about Jesus is banned from going to worship ever again. [*To Simon*] Seth's a big boy now. Ask him.
Narrator	And he took his wife's arm and hurried quickly away.
Simon	[*To Seth*] Come on, admit it – Jesus is a crook, isn't he?
Seth	That's not for me to say, but I do know that once I was blind, and now I can see. And if it comes to that, I can see the blindingly obvious when it's right in front of me, which is more than you can, and you reckon you're *not* blind! It's all those precious rules – you can't see past them!
Simon	[*Angrily*] Oh, you're a bad lot – you always have been. You were born bad, and bad is what you'll always be. Never darken the door of my synagogue again.
Seth	Suits me. My eyes have been opened to see what's good. I don't want to end up blind to it again, like you. Now, where's this Jesus fellow got to – I think it's time we had a word.

In the Church's beginning, God . . . _____

The gift of the Holy Spirit

Preparation page

What's the point?

The Holy Spirit, at Pentecost, empowered the disciples with the resources they needed for their time and place. Like Moses, they were given the ability to go and communicate God's word. The barriers of language were broken down and the gospel began to be heard.

Preparation

Make some 'flash cards'. Ask the young people of the church for examples of words or phrases that their parents either don't understand, or understand differently. Examples might be computer terminology, or simply words that have become applied as slang – at the time of writing, for example, 'wicked' might mean something radically different in the playground culture from in the church! Divide a sheet of paper into eight equal sections by folding it, and then write in large letters in each section one of the words or phrases. On a second sheet of paper, write the meanings in a similar fashion. Then photocopy the pages on to different coloured cards – one colour for the buzz-words and another for the interpretations. You will need enough cards for each worshipper to be given one, of whichever colour comes to hand, as they enter the church, and a complete set for yourself.

Suggested songs

God is here, God is present
Hang on, stand still, stay put, hold tight
I'm so excited
Jesus, send me the helper
You've got to move when the Spirit says move

Checklist

At the service, you will need:

- the flash cards
- your complete set
- Blu-Tack or pins

All-age worship

Opening song

A song praising and celebrating the faithfulness of God

Prayer

Loving God,
we meet here like your friends so long ago,
praying that you will pour out your Spirit on us
and give us the gifts of faith we need
to be your people in the world.
Please forgive us for the lack of commitment we sometimes feel,
and give us confidence to go from here full of joy,
to tell your Good News to the world.
Amen.

Word and action

Action

Get the stewards to give the cards to worshippers as they arrive, and then hand any remaining cards to you as the service begins. Now, check that everyone has a card and ask them to pair them up. They will need to talk to one another, comparing cards, to see whether they can pair up a word with its meaning. If they get really stuck, you have the leftover cards and can help.

Although they will obviously begin by comparing with the people immediately around them, at least some people will need to get up and move to a different place, to consult more widely. After a due time, call people to order and go through your own full set of cards. Pin up each word in turn and see whether the congregation can now give you its meaning, at which point you can pin the interpretation alongside the word.

You can then point out that if the church is to communicate with present-day culture, it is going to have to make this kind of an effort. We can and should pray for the gifts we need, but we also know that the Holy Spirit often works through the company of God's people. So is he calling us to listen more carefully to one another, and especially to those whose language seems different, in an attempt to understand and communicate?

Now, read the story – either as narrative or drama.

Word: Acts 2:1-12
God breaks the language barrier

(See page 69 for a dramatised version of this story.)

The friends of Jesus had a wonderful story to tell. For a time, they'd thought it was all over – the people who hated Jesus had had him killed, but what do you think had happened after that?* God raised him from the dead and gave him new life – and he'd been seen by all his close friends before he went back to heaven. But they had a promise that he'd always be with them, and he'd told them to tell the whole world the Good News that he was alive.

* Well, what *do* they think happened?

'So what are we waiting for?' Peter was grumbling. 'We've got to do as Jesus said – tell the world. And instead we're all sitting here together just praying!'

Peter always was the one who went at everything like a bull at a gate – head down, mouth in gear, brain in neutral! 'Jesus also told us,' Andrew reminded him, 'to wait until we get the power we need. I don't know what he meant, but I'm sure we'll know when we get it.'

'But we're missing the boat,' Peter objected. 'This is the great festival – there are people from all over the world here, and we've got to tell them so they can go home and tell their friends.'

'Fine,' Thomas chipped in. 'And just how are you going to talk to foreign visitors when none of us can speak any of their languages?'

Peter had to admit Thomas had a point – but before he could answer something really strange started happening. It was a sound like a gale blowing through the room – but the air was completely still. The sound got louder and louder – everyone was waiting for the roof to come off the house, but still they didn't feel anything.

Philip, another of the friends, knew something important was going on. 'Didn't Jesus say that God's Spirit was like the wind?' he said. 'Didn't he say something about it blowing and you never knew where it came from or where it went?'

'Oh, heaven save us, he's getting all intellectual!' Peter knew all about nets and fish, but he would never have called himself a deep thinker.

'He's right, though,' Nathanael chipped in. 'That's exactly what Jesus said, and it's *exactly* what's happening now.'

'Never mind all the fancy theories,' Peter snapped. 'We've got to get out there and *do* something. On second thoughts,' his voice took on a panicky note, 'just get out – the room's on fire!'

'You know,' said Philip, calmly, 'I do believe he's right – the room *is* on fire. This is very interesting.'

'Never mind interesting – let's get out!'

'But it's not burning, is it?' Philip mused. 'The room's full of fire, but nothing's getting burnt.'

He was right. Gradually the panic subsided, but Peter was still agitated. 'What's going on?' he said. 'I can't remember anything like this before.'

'Yes you can,' Philip corrected him. 'Moses – the burning bush – it was on fire but it never got burnt. Don't you see?'

Peter didn't see. But Nathanael did.

'This is the power Jesus promised us!' he exclaimed. 'Just like Moses – God's giving us the power we need to go and do his work. Oh, I say – where's everybody gone?'

When Nathanael went outside he saw the most amazing scene. There was Peter, rattling on nineteen to the dozen – well, there was nothing strange in that but he was talking Arabic – telling someone from Libya all about Jesus. Then he heard Andrew's voice – but Andrew was speaking in Latin, and he'd never been any good at that – and yet he'd buttonholed a Roman merchant who just couldn't wait to hear more.

Just as he was trying to take all this in, a woman came up to him and said, 'What's this all about?'

'I'm really very sorry,' Nathanael answered without stopping to think, 'but I don't speak Turkish. You'll have to ask someone else.'

The woman looked bemused. 'I don't understand,' she said.

'Well, it's really simple enough,' Nathanael said, a little crossly. 'I don't speak your language – go and ask someone who does.'

The woman smiled. 'If you don't speak my language, how come I'm understanding every word you're saying?'

She was right! Everyone was amazed. The Good News about Jesus was being spread to all the foreign visitors *in their own languages*. 'Well!' said Nathanael. 'So this is what God's Holy Spirit can do. Impressive. *Very* impressive!'

Song 2

Offering

This may be introduced as a sign of our willingness to offer ourselves to God so that he can equip and use us to offer a new beginning to the world – starting with ourselves!

Offertory prayer

Loving God, you give us so much –
accept what we offer here as a sign of our gratitude,
but also of our faith
as we respond to your invitation to be your people in the world.
Amen.

Song 3

Reading

John 13:34-35 read from a standard Bible. Introduce it with words such as: As he offers us a new beginning, Jesus gives us a new commandment. And he makes it sound so simple!

Talk (optional)

If you feel it appropriate (and if time permits) you can comment that Jesus' new commandment puts all the other stories into perspective. There is no point-scoring here, but just a burning desire that the love of Jesus should be known and enjoyed by all people.

Notices and family news

Prayers of intercession

Song 4

Closing prayer/benediction

Dramatised reading
God breaks the language barrier

Narrator	The friends of Jesus had a wonderful story to tell. For a time, they'd thought it was all over – the people who hated Jesus had had him killed, but God raised him from the dead and gave him new life – and he'd been seen by all his close friends before he went back to heaven. But they had a promise that he'd always be with them, and he'd told them to tell the whole world the Good News that he was alive – and Peter was getting impatient.
Peter	So what are we waiting for? We've got to do as he said – tell the world. And instead we're all sitting here together just praying!
Narrator	Peter always was the one who went at everything like a bull at a gate – head down, mouth in gear, brain in neutral!
Andrew	Jesus also told us to wait until we get the power we need. I don't know what he meant, but I'm sure we'll know when we get it.
Peter	But, Andrew, this is the great festival – there are people from all over the world here, and we've got to tell them so they can go home and tell their friends. That's right, isn't it, Thomas?
Thomas	Fine – and just how are you going to talk to foreign visitors when none of us can speak any of their languages?
Narrator	Peter had to admit Thomas had a point – but before he could answer, something really strange started happening. It sounded like a gale blowing through the room – but the air was completely still. It got louder and louder, but still they didn't feel anything. Philip, another of the friends, knew something important was going on.
Philip	Didn't Jesus say that God's Spirit was like the wind? Didn't he say something about it blowing and you never knew where it came from or where it went?
Peter	Oh, heaven save us, he's getting all intellectual!
Narrator	Peter knew all about nets and fish, but he would never have called himself a deep thinker.
Nathanael	He's right, though – that's exactly what Jesus said, and it's *exactly* what's happening now.
Peter	Never mind the theories, Nathanael. We've got to get out and *do* something. On second thoughts, just get out – the room's on fire!
Philip	[*Calmly*] You know, I do believe he's right – the room *is* on fire. This is very interesting.
Peter	Never mind interesting – let's get out!
Philip	But it's not burning, is it? Lots of fire, but nothing's burning.
Narrator	He was right. Gradually the panic subsided, but Peter was still agitated.

Peter	What's going on? I can't remember anything like this before.
Philip	Yes you can. Moses – the burning bush – it was on fire but it never got burnt. Don't you see?
Narrator	Peter didn't see. But Nathanael did.
Nathanael	This is the Holy Spirit Jesus promised us! Just like Moses – God's giving us the power we need to go and do his work. Oh, I say – where's everybody gone?
Narrator	When Nathanael went outside he was amazed. Peter was rattling on nineteen to the dozen – nothing strange in that but he was telling someone from Libya about Jesus – in Arabic. Then he heard Andrew speaking Latin – he'd buttonholed a Roman merchant who just couldn't wait to hear more. Just then, a woman came up to Nathanael.
Woman	What's this all about?
Nathanael	I'm really very sorry, but I don't speak Turkish. You'll have to ask someone else.
Woman	I don't understand.
Nathanael	Well, it's really simple enough: I don't speak your language – go and ask someone who does.
Woman	If you don't speak my language, how come I'm understanding every word you're saying?
Narrator	She was right! Everyone was amazed. The Good News about Jesus was being spread to all the foreign visitors *in their own languages*.
Nathanael	So this is God's Holy Spirit at work. Impressive. *Very* impressive.

From trouble to triumph

Joseph: From prisoner to governor of Egypt ___

Preparation page

What's the point?

It wasn't easy – no snap-of-the-fingers quick fix – but out of Joseph's life God brought a great result. However, while it wasn't a quick fix, it wasn't a case of 'just sit back and wait', either. A number of different people played their part. So we need not only to trust God to bring good out of trouble but be alert to how he might be hoping to use us in the process.

Preparation

Think about a modern-day situation where someone is in trouble and needs to be rescued. What different characters would need to be involved? For example, in the case of a mountain rescue, the police might be alerted first, and then call in the mountain rescue team, who might use a tracker dog to locate the victim in the snow. They'd need a trained first-aider or perhaps a paramedic on hand to give any necessary on-the-spot treatment, and possibly a helicopter pilot and helicopter winchman to airlift the victim to hospital where a team of doctors and nurses would take over. Of course, you could go on and on, but try to keep focused on just the basic team. Write their titles on a sheet of paper, photocopy several times and then cut into separate cards, each bearing the title of one of the team.

Suggested songs

God cares for all creation
Let us sing your glory, Lord
Lord, the light of your love is shining
Safe in the Father's hands
So I'll trust

Checklist

For the service, you will need:

* the cards – probably best given out with the hymn books at the door
* an overhead projector or poster with the full team list on it

All-age worship

Opening song

A song praising and celebrating the faithfulness of God

Prayer

Thank you, loving God, for caring so much for each of us.
Thank you for the people you put us with,
and the opportunities you give us to serve you in often unexpected ways.
Please forgive us for the times
when we forget about your blessings or each other's needs,
and help us to live together as your people,
open to the special gifts each one of us has.
Through Jesus Christ our Lord.
Amen.

Word and action

Action

Have the cards randomly given out as people arrive at the church. At this point in the service, divide the congregation into groups and ask them to imagine your hypothetical rescue situation. They are to assemble a team from the cards they have, and the personnel needed are listed on the overhead or board. Undoubtedly, no group will start out with the right combination of cards, and they will need to swap around the church (encourage them to move around freely) in order to assemble their team. There will also be some cards left over, but to save time stress that each group need only assemble one team. If you like, you could speed things up by making it a competition and stopping when the first team is formed.

You can now simply point out that in order for this single mission to be accomplished a kind of jigsaw puzzle of skills and resources had to be completed. God worked a bit like that in the story of Joseph, and we're now going to hear the final part of that story in which the pieces eventually came together.

Word: Genesis 41
Joseph the governor

(See page 77 for a dramatised version of this story.)

Pharaoh, the king of Egypt, was not happy. 'What do I pay all these magicians and mumbo-jumboers for,' he grumbled, 'if when I want just a little thing like to be told what my dreams mean, no one can do it?'

Corky, the palace wine waiter, suddenly remembered something important he'd forgotten to tell Pharaoh.

'You remember that time when you put me in prison?' he said. 'Well, I met this Hebrew slave there – Joseph, or Jonah, or something, he was called. Seems he'd been put in there when someone told whoppers about him, but he won the trust of the jailer and ended up being put in charge of the other prisoners. Anyway, when I had a strange dream, he told me what it meant. And he was right, too. Anyway, I just thought you might be interested. Now, I've got this nice drop of wine for you . . .'

'Never mind the wine,' said Pharaoh, impatiently, 'get me this Joel character, or whatever his name is.'

Joseph was feeling a bit down that morning. 'I don't know what God's up to,' he was saying. 'When my brothers sold me for a slave I thought I'd had it – then I ended up here in Egypt and became the trusted senior slave of a VIP, and thought maybe things weren't so bad after all. Then what happens? His wife goes and tells a pack of lies and I end up in here.'

'Well,' said the jailer, 'your luck may be changing – Pharaoh wants to see you.'

'What!' exclaimed Joseph. 'Go and see Pharaoh? But I look awful.'

'Never mind that,' the guard growled at him. 'You'll look a sight worse if you argue – now get along.'

So Pharaoh told Joseph all about his strange dream.

'I was standing by the river meditating – the way you do – when these seven big, fat cows came up out of the river. "Well," I thought, "they've been well fed." And even as I thought it, these seven other cows came up as well – really thin, and ugly. Then, while I was watching, what d'you think happened? The seven thin, ugly cows gobbled up the seven fat ones. Just like that – bones and all. That did it – I woke up. Well, you would, wouldn't you?'

'I think I can help with that,' Joseph began.

'You'll speak when you're spoken to,' Pharaoh interrupted. 'I haven't finished yet. I went back to sleep, and dreamed about these seven ears of corn – really good, ripe corn. Then these seven other ears of corn sprang up – all thin and weak, and not the sort of thing you'd feed to your pet pooch. And guess what happened then? The seven thin ears of corn swallowed the ripe ears all up. OK, that's it. Talk. And make it good – I hear you're spot on with this sort of thing. So what does it mean?'

'Well, it's not really me, Your Majesty,' Joseph answered. 'It's God who tells me what these things mean. Think of the cows and the ears of wheat as years. You've got seven good years coming, when the farming will do really well. But then you're going to have seven terrible years – and all the goodness of the first seven years will be completely swallowed up by the bad ones.'

Pharaoh was horrified. 'But what can we do?' he cried.

'What you need, Your Majesty,' Joseph told him, 'is a really good governor: someone seriously wise and clever – and who listens to what God says – who can manage the good years, and save as much food as possible to see you through the bad ones. Of course, where you find a guy like that's another matter.'

'Seems to me I'm looking at him,' Pharaoh said. 'Right, you're it. Whatever you say goes from now on. No one in Egypt's greater than you – except me, of course. Well, what are you waiting for? Get managing.'

Joseph did a really good job. He had big storehouses built, and every bit of food that wasn't strictly needed was saved. Then, seven years later, when the bad years came – just as God had told him they would – there was food for all the people. And when the famine spread worldwide, people from other nations soon realised there was food in Egypt, and started coming to Joseph to buy some. And it wasn't long before Joseph's father Jacob heard about it. Of course, he didn't know it was Joseph who was the brains behind it – he thought Joseph was long dead – but he heard there was food there, and he called his sons to him.

'I want you to go to Egypt, and find this governor fellow, and buy some food. And don't come back here without it.'

So, of course, you can guess what happened. To cut a very long story short, Jacob was overjoyed to find that Joseph was alive after all – and not only alive but a very important person in Egypt – and the whole family went to live with him there. 'Trust God,' Jacob said, 'to bring something good out of all that trouble!'

Song 2

Offering

This may be introduced as our offering of ourselves and our resources for God to use in his redemptive work.

Offertory prayer

Loving God, we thank you for your gift of grace,
able to bring good out of any difficulties.
We offer you our small gifts,
that people now experiencing dark and difficult times
may know the promise of your love.
Amen.

Song 3

Reading

Romans 8:35-39, read from a standard Bible. Introduce it with words such as: Paul declares his faith that nothing – absolutely nothing – can ever separate us from God's love – something that Joseph would certainly have agreed with.

Talk (optional)

It's rather important to say here that this kind of faith does not mean we belittle people's troubles or question the faith of people who despair. Rather, it means that *our* faith gives us genuine hope which allows us to share their troubles without resorting to easy clichés.

Notices and family news

Prayers of intercession

Song 4

Closing prayer/benediction

Dramatised reading
Joseph the governor

Pharaoh   What's the point of being Pharaoh, if when I want just a little thing like to be told what my dreams mean, no one can do it?

Narrator   Corky, the palace wine waiter, suddenly remembered something he'd forgotten.

Corky   You remember that time when you put me in prison? Well, I met this Hebrew slave there – Joseph, or Jonah, or something, he was called. Seems he'd been put in there when someone told whoppers about him, but he won the trust of the jailer and ended up being put in charge of the other prisoners. Anyway, when I had a strange dream, he told me what it meant. And he was right, too. Just thought you might be interested.

Pharaoh   Get me this Joel, or whatever his name is.

Narrator   Joseph was feeling a bit down that morning.

Joseph   I don't know what God's up to. When my brothers sold me as a slave I thought I'd had it – then I ended up here in Egypt and became the trusted senior slave of a VIP, and things weren't so bad after all. Then what happens? His wife goes and tells a pack of lies and I end up in here.

Guard   Well, your luck may be changing – I've just heard Pharaoh wants to see you.

Joseph   What? Go and see Pharaoh? But I look awful!

Guard   Never mind that. You'll look a sight worse if you argue – now get along.

Narrator   So Pharaoh told Joseph all about his strange dream.

Pharaoh   I was standing by the river meditating – the way you do – when these seven fat cows came up out of the river. 'Well,' I thought, 'they've been well fed.' And just then, these seven other cows came up as well – really thin, and ugly. And while I was watching, what d'you think happened? The seven thin, ugly cows gobbled up the seven fat ones. Just like that – bones and all. Well, that did it – I woke up. Well, you would, wouldn't you? Anyway, I went back to sleep, and dreamed about these seven ears of corn – really good, ripe corn. Then these seven other ears of corn sprang up – all thin and weak, and not the sort of thing you'd feed to your pet pooch. And guess what happened then? The seven thin ears of corn swallowed the ripe ears all up. OK, that's it. Talk. And make it good – I hear you're spot on with this sort of thing. So what does it mean?

Joseph   Well, it's not really me, Your Majesty. It's God who tells me what these things mean. Think of the cows and the wheat as years. You'll have seven good years, when the farming will do really well, and then seven terrible years – and all the goodness of the first seven years will be completely swallowed up by the bad ones.

Pharaoh   [*Horrified*] But what can we do?

Joseph   What you need, Your Majesty, is a really good governor: someone seriously wise and clever – and who listens to what God says – who can manage the good years, and save as much food as possible to see you through the bad ones. Of course, where you find a guy like that's another matter.

Pharaoh   Seems to me I'm looking at him. Right, whatever you say goes from now on. No one in Egypt's greater than you – except me, of course. Well, what are you waiting for? Get managing.

Narrator   Joseph had big storehouses built, and every bit of food that wasn't strictly needed was saved. Then, seven years later, when the bad years came – just as God had told him they would – there was food for all the people. And when the famine spread worldwide, people from other nations soon realised there was food in Egypt, and started coming to Joseph to buy some. And it wasn't long before Joseph's father Jacob heard about it. Of course, he didn't know it was Joseph who was the brains behind it – he thought Joseph was long dead – but he heard there was food there, and he called his sons to him.

Jacob   I want you to go to Egypt, and find this governor fellow, and buy some food. And don't come back here without it.

Narrator   So, of course, you can guess what happened. To cut a very long story short, Jacob was overjoyed to find that Joseph was alive after all – and not only alive but a very important person in Egypt – and the whole family went to live with him there.

Jacob   Trust God to bring something good out of all that trouble!

Israel in Babylon:
From military defeat to moral victory_____

Shadrach, Meshach and Abednego

Preparation page

What's the point?

Babylon might have had all the military power, but that doesn't have the final word. Ultimately, ideas and beliefs are stronger than weapons and the moral victory is still there to be fought for and won.

Preparation

Create a display of important social accessories or identifiers (you could ask the young people for ideas as to what to include, but mobile phones and designer clothes would be two obvious items). Cut out pictures from magazines, or get some actual examples.

Write the following texts in large print on two separate pieces of A4 paper: 'Choose this day whom you will serve', and 'We will serve the Lord'. (It's a cut-down version of Joshua 24:15.) Finally, photocopy each sheet on to a different colour card, and cut up so that each word is on a separate card. You will need enough copies for each worshipper to be given one word of each colour.

Suggested songs

Father, I place into your hands
How great is our God
Hey, now, everybody sing
I'm gonna click, click, click
Lift his name high
Sing and shout your praise to our God

Checklist

At the service you will need:
- the display, set up at the front
- the cards for distribution at the door.
- Blu-Tack

All-age worship

Opening song

A song praising and celebrating the faithfulness of God

Prayer

Loving God, we're here to worship you
and thank you for all the good things you give us.
We enjoy the good things that are around us,
but sometimes they get a bit out of proportion.
Please forgive us when we make idols out of things and forget you,
and help us always to keep you at the centre of our lives.
Amen.

Word and action

Action

Have the individual word cards given out at random as the congregation enter the church. Each person should be given one of each colour.

Now, draw attention to the display and reflect briefly on how easy it is to become idolatrous, just in an understandable attempt not to be different. The trouble is that different is exactly what God calls us to be – as the characters in this story knew. At this stage, read the story.

Word: Daniel 3
God's resistance

(See page 83 for a dramatised version of this story.)

This is the story of Shadrach, Meshach and Abednego.*

It was a hot day in Babylon – every day was a hot day in Babylon, but this one was about to get hotter because King Nebuchadnezzar had had one of his silly ideas. 'Everyone must worship this statue of me,' said King Nebuchadnezzar, 'because it's beautiful – well, it would be, wouldn't it? And anyone who doesn't want to worship this statue of me will be burned in the burning fiery furnace – so there!'

The statue was over 25 metres high, and made of solid gold. 'And I'm worth every ounce of it,' said Nebuchadnezzar, 'because I'm the bestest king what ever was, and I write poems, like, you know.' Then he started chanting. 'Worship me, worship me, or I'll burn you horribly. When you hear the trumpets blowing, bow your heads and let's get going. When you hear the drummers bashing, hit the deck and say I'm smashing.'

In the crowd were Shadrach, Meshach and Abednego. They were Jewish men, captured by King Nebuchadnezzar when he conquered Jerusalem – and they weren't impressed. 'It's enough to make you *cringe*,' said Shadrach, 'but I'm certainly not going to *bow* – not to that great big pile of rubbish, and not to his statue either.'

---

* Actually, the names are quite rhythmic, aren't they. Would the children enjoy saying them a few times? A fun way of telling the story would be to get the children to join in with them. Every time you say all three names together, ask, 'Who?' and let the children repeat them.

King Nebuchadnezzar was just getting into his stride. 'Come and praise me, everybody; I'm your king and I'm your god-ee.'

Even Nebuchadnezzar himself looked a bit embarrassed by that one. The bandmaster decided someone had to do something about it, and started the music. Everybody bowed down. Everybody except Shadrach, Meshach and Abednego.

'I'm standing up for the one true God,' said Shadrach.

'Me too,' added Meshach.

'Me five,' said Abednego.

'Really, Abednego,' exclaimed Meshach, 'when are you going to learn to count!'

'A bit late for that, I think,' Abednego answered. 'The king doesn't look too pleased.'

Nebuchadnezzar was dancing up and down with rage. And his dancing was even worse than his poetry. 'Bow down!' he screamed at them. 'Bow down and worship my statue.'

'Well, thank goodness he's stopped doing silly rhymes, anyway,' said Abednego.

The king went on. 'If you don't bow, I'm going to burn you. You need a lesson and I'm going to learn you.'

The burning fiery furnace seemed almost a relief after that. The soldiers opened the door and pushed Shadrach, Meshach and Abednego in. Hot? You've never felt anything like it – and they hadn't got a factor 35 between them.

Outside the furnace, the king was still carrying on. 'Everybody, sing my praises, or like them you'll go to blazes.'

Before he could get even worse he stopped and looked through the furnace window, and couldn't believe his eyes.

'I say,' he said to his chief adviser, 'didn't we put three men into the fire to burn?'

'Yes, Your Majesty, I counted them all in.'

King Nebuchadnezzar looked worried. 'Then why are there four of them in there now, and why are they walking about, and why does one of them look like some kind of a god? Oh, my . . . word! Get them out! Get them out!'

The door was opened, and out came Shadrach, Meshach and Abednego, and there wasn't a singed hair between them.

Nebuchadnezzar decided it was time to get sensible. 'No more golden statues,' he said. 'From now on we worship the God of Shadrach, Meshach and Abednego.'

And everyone agreed. And they were all very pleased. Especially Shadrach, Meshach and Abednego.

Action

Get the congregation to work together – you might find it easier to divide them into groups – to reconstruct the text you have given them. No word is repeated on the same colour of card, so they can start by just swapping duplicates and then see if they can see the text emerging. The first group to finish and assemble the text correctly can then come and Blu-Tack their cards over the display of 'idols'. If they get really stuck, tell them where the text is from.

Song 2

Offering

This may be introduced as a symbol of our commitment to keeping God at the centre of our lives.

Offertory prayer

Lord God, thank you for always being at the heart of our lives.
Help us to use the gifts you give us, and offer them to you,
so that the world may recognise that, also.
Amen.

Song 3

Reading

Matthew 4:1-11 read from a standard Bible. Introduce it with words such as: Even Jesus was tempted to turn away from God, misuse his power and idolise the ways of the world.

Talk (optional)

If you feel it appropriate (and if time permits) you can point out that the basic temptations are very similar in all times and places: to allow worldly fame, wealth and power to usurp the true God. Babylon might have won the military battle, but the moral victory was with God's people. And, just in case we start getting the wrong ideas about that, it was *God's* power, not theirs, that won it!

Notices and family news

Prayers of intercession

Song 4

Closing prayer/benediction

Dramatised reading
God's resistance

Narrator	It was a hot day in Babylon – every day was a hot day in Babylon, but this one was about to get hotter because King Nebuchadnezzar had had one of his silly ideas.
Nebuchadnezzar	Everyone must worship this statue of me because it's beautiful – well, it would be, wouldn't it? And anyone who doesn't want to worship this statue of me will be burned in the burning fiery furnace – so there!
Narrator	The statue was over 25 metres high, and made of solid gold.
Nebuchadnezzar	And I'm worth every ounce of it, because I'm the bestest king what ever was, and I write poems, like, you know. [Chants] Worship me, worship me, or I'll burn you horribly. When you hear the trumpets blowing, bow your heads and let's get going. When you hear the drummers bashing, hit the deck and say I'm smashing.
Narrator	In the crowd were Shadrach, Meshach and Abednego. They were Jewish men, captured by King Nebuchadnezzar when he conquered Jerusalem – and they weren't impressed.
Shadrach	It's enough to make you cringe, but I'm certainly not going to bow – not to that great big pile of rubbish, and not to his statue either.
Narrator	King Nebuchadnezzar was just getting into his stride.
Nebuchadnezzar	Come and praise me, everybody; I'm your king and I'm your god–ee.
Narrator	Even Nebuchadnezzar himself looked a bit embarrassed by that one. The bandmaster decided someone had to do something about it, and started the music. Everybody bowed down. Everybody except Shadrach, Meshach and Abednego.
Shadrach	I'm standing up for the one true God.
Meshach	Me too.
Abednego	Me five.
Meshach	Really, Abednego! When are you going to learn to count!
Abednego	A bit late for that, I think. The king doesn't look too pleased.
Narrator	Nebuchadnezzar was dancing up and down with rage. And his dancing was even worse than his poetry.
Nebuchadnezzar	Bow down! Bow down and worship my statue.
Abednego	Well, thank goodness he's stopped doing silly rhymes, anyway.

Nebuchadnezzar	If you don't bow, I'm going to burn you. You need a lesson and I'm going to learn you.
Narrator	Well, the burning fiery furnace seemed almost a relief after that. The soldiers opened the door and pushed Shadrach, Meshach and Abednego in. Hot? You've never felt anything like it – and they hadn't got a factor 35 between them. Outside the furnace, the king was still carrying on.
Nebuchadnezzar	Everybody, sing my praises, or like them you'll go to blazes.
Narrator	Before he could get even worse he stopped and looked through the furnace window, and couldn't believe his eyes. He called his chief adviser.
Nebuchadnezzar	I say, didn't we put *three* men into the fire to burn?
Adviser	Yes, Your Majesty, I counted them all in.
Nebuchadnezzar	Then why are there four of them in there now, and why are they walking about, and why does one of them look like some kind of a god? Oh, my . . . word! Get them out! Get them out!
Narrator	The door was opened, and out came Shadrach, Meshach and Abednego, and there wasn't a singed hair between them. Nebuchadnezzar decided it was time to get sensible.
Nebuchadnezzar	No more golden statues. From now on we worship the God of Shadrach, Meshach and Abednego.
Narrator	And everyone agreed. And they were all very pleased. Especially Shadrach, Meshach and Abednego.

Jesus: From despair to hope

Jesus appears to his disciples at Emmaus

Preparation page

What's the point?

Sometimes people who are finding life tough aren't able to see that Christ is with them. Often it's a simple act of sharing that makes him 'visible'.

Preparation

On a number of paper plates, write the words 'Jesus is here' – ensuring that the pen you are using is non-toxic! To be doubly safe you could use food colouring, with proper cake-decorating brushes. Then, in time for the service, buy some biscuits to pass round on the plates.

Suggested songs

Break the bread and pour the wine
Brother, sister, let me serve you
Jesus put this song into our hearts
Walk in the light
We are marching in the light of God
You shall go out with joy

Checklist

At the service, you will need:
• the plates, with the biscuits already on them

All-age worship

Opening Song

A song praising and celebrating the faithfulness of God

Prayer

Loving God, we thank and praise you for your love,
stronger than fear and even death itself.
We thank you for being with your people
even when we don't recognise you.
Forgive us for the times
when our own actions and attitudes obscure your presence,
and help us to live so that others may recognise you.
Through Jesus Christ our Lord.
Amen.

Word and action

Action

Get the children to pass out the biscuits on the specially prepared plates. Ask the congregation to let you know when they get the point of it: the act of sharing has revealed Christ's presence.

Word: Luke 24:13-35
Walking from despair to hope

(See page 89 for a dramatised version of this story.)

Cleopas and Judith were friends of Jesus – and they were terribly upset.

'I know Jesus offended a lot of people,' Judith said, 'but they had no reason to have him killed – and in a horrible way like that, as well.'

'He was too honest, that was his trouble,' Cleopas observed. 'Anyway, I don't like Jerusalem any more – let's go home to Emmaus.'

'Good idea,' Judith agreed. 'Let's get away from all these horrible memories.'

So they set out to walk to Emmaus, about seven miles away, and as they walked they tried to make sense of what had happened.

'He was such a good man,' Cleopas said. 'It just doesn't add up.'

'I thought he was the special man God had promised,' Judith added, 'but if he was, why did God let him be killed?'

'Don't look now,' Cleopas whispered, 'but we're not alone.'

He was right – a mysterious figure was catching up with them. 'What are you talking about?' the man asked.

Cleopas and Judith stopped and stared. 'You mean you don't know?' Judith gasped. 'Are you the only person who's been in Jerusalem this weekend and doesn't know what's happened?'

'Why?' asked the stranger. 'What *has* happened?'

'Oh, nothing much,' sniffed Judith, tearfully. 'They've just gone and killed Jesus, that's all, and after all the wonderful things he did, as well.'

'Yes,' Cleopas added, 'and we were thinking he was the great promised Messiah.'

'That was on Friday,' Judith said, 'and now there are all kinds of rumours going round. Some of our friends went to his grave this morning and came back saying that he'd risen – said they'd seen some angels who'd told them so.'

'Women, you know,' said Cleopas. 'No one else saw anything.'

The stranger spoke kindly, but sounded disappointed. 'When are you going to learn to listen to the prophets?' he said. 'Wasn't all this foretold, that the Messiah would be treated badly, but then God would glorify him?' And before they could stop him he was giving them an off-the-cuff Bible study. They hardly noticed the miles as they listened to him, and before they knew it they were at Emmaus. The stranger was still in full flood, but when they got to their door he stopped. 'Well, I'll say goodnight,' he said.

'Oh, you can't!' exclaimed Judith. 'Look, it's getting dark – why don't you come and stay with us?'

'That's kind of you,' said the stranger, and they went into the house.

'Not much for supper, I'm afraid,' Cleopas apologised. 'We weren't expecting to be home tonight, so the neighbours won't have got anything in for us. We can manage a bit of bread and wine, though.'

'That sounds terrific,' answered the stranger. 'You'd be amazed what you can do with a bit of bread and wine.'

Soon, they had a roaring fire going to keep them warm and the room was beginning to look almost cheerful in spite of everything. They sat down to eat, and Cleopas reached out to take the bread and hand it round, but the stranger got there first. He took the bread, and he said grace, and then, gripping the loaf between his hands, he broke it. 'Here you are,' he said. 'Take and eat this.'

Suddenly, a shiver went down Cleopas's spine. It was as though they were back in that room where they'd shared their last supper with Jesus before he'd been killed. Something about the way he said grace . . . and broke the bread . . . and offered it to them. Cleopas looked at Judith, and knew she'd felt it, too. The same tingle, the same flash of recognition. Their eyes met, and lit up with joy. 'It's him!' they chorused, and together they reached out to take Jesus' hands. Laughing and crying at the same time, with joy, they grasped hold of . . . nothing. He wasn't there any more.

'Of course!' laughed Judith. 'He's alive, and he's free, and he's not to be clutched or held or pinned down by anybody ever again.'

They didn't say any more, but got up and dashed back to Jerusalem – all seven miles of it. 'This is the place to be!' said Cleopas. 'This is where God's bringing new hope out of all that pain.' And he was right.

Action

Remind the congregation of the activity, in which the action of sharing revealed the presence of Christ. You can then elaborate further: the two disciples were having a dreadfully troubled time, and thought Jesus wasn't with them any more. Even when he was there, they couldn't recognise him, but *in the act of sharing* his presence was made clear. Maybe there are people today in their position – so troubled that all they can think of is getting away from whatever it is, and unable to see that Christ is walking with them. So who is going to share their journey, their story? And most importantly, who by sharing friendship is going to help them recognise that Christ is still with them?

Song 2

Offering

This may be introduced as our contribution to God's mission of hope and redemption.

Offertory prayer

Loving God, we thank you for the rich gifts that you give us,
and especially for the gift of hope in your Son Jesus Christ.
Here we offer ourselves and our gifts for you to use
that others may also know your hope.
Through Jesus Christ our Lord.
Amen.

Song 3

Reading

Isaiah 30:15-18 read from a standard Bible. Introduce it with words such as: The prophet tells God's people who are in trouble not to panic but to rely on God.

Talk (optional)

If you feel it appropriate (and if time permits) you can sum up by saying that God's way of dealing with trouble is to bring hope from within the situation itself. The two disciples learnt that it was at the very place where the pain was – the place from which they were trying to get away – that God would bring new hope. But Christ's way of showing that was to share their journey, even though they were going the wrong way!

Notices and family news

Prayers of intercession

Song 4

Closing prayer/benediction

Dramatised reading
Walking from despair to hope

Narrator	Cleopas and Judith were friends of Jesus – and they were terribly upset.
Judith	I know Jesus offended a lot of people, but they had no reason to have him killed – and in a horrible way like that, as well.
Cleopas	He was too honest, that was his trouble. Anyway, I don't like Jerusalem any more – let's go home to Emmaus.
Judith	Good idea. Let's get away from all these horrible memories.
Narrator	So they set out to walk to Emmaus, about seven miles away, and as they walked they tried to make sense of what had happened.
Cleopas	He was such a good man. It just doesn't add up.
Judith	I thought he was the special man God had promised, but if he was, why did God let him be killed?
Cleopas	Don't look now, but we're not alone.
Narrator	He was right – a mysterious figure was catching up with them.
Jesus	What are you talking about?
Judith	You mean you don't know? Are you the only person who's been in Jerusalem this weekend and doesn't know what's happened?
Jesus	Why? What *has* happened?
Judith	Oh, nothing much – they've just gone and killed Jesus, that's all, and after all the wonderful things he did, as well.
Cleopas	Yes, and we were thinking he was the great promised Messiah.
Judith	That was Friday, and now all kinds of rumours are going round. Some of our friends went to his grave this morning and came back saying that he'd risen – some angels had told them so.
Cleopas	Women, you know. No one else saw anything.
Narrator	The stranger spoke kindly, but sounded disappointed.
Jesus	When are you going to listen to the prophets? Wasn't it foretold that the Messiah would suffer, but then God would glorify him?
Narrator	Before they could stop him the stranger was giving them an off-the-cuff Bible study. They hardly noticed the miles as they listened to him, and soon they were at Emmaus. The stranger was still in full flood, but when they got to their door he stopped.
Jesus	Well, I'll say goodnight.
Judith	Look, it's getting dark – why don't you come and stay with us?
Cleopas	Not much for supper, I'm afraid – we weren't expecting to be home tonight. We can manage a bit of bread and wine, though.
Jesus	That sounds terrific. You'd be amazed what you can do with a bit of bread and wine.
Narrator	They sat down to eat, and Cleopas reached out to take the

	bread and hand it round, but the stranger got there first. He took the bread, and he said grace, and then, gripping the loaf between his hands, he broke it.
Jesus	Here you are – take and eat this.
Narrator	Suddenly, a shiver went down Cleopas's spine. It was as though they were back in that room where they'd shared their last supper with Jesus before he'd been killed. Something about the way he said grace . . . and broke the bread . . . and offered it to them. Cleopas looked at Judith, and knew she'd felt it, too. The same tingle, the same flash of recognition. Their eyes met, and lit up with joy.
Judith and Cleopas	It's him!
Narrator	Together they reached out to take Jesus' hands. Laughing and crying at the same time, with joy, they grasped hold of . . . nothing. He wasn't there any more.
Judith	Of course! He's alive, and he's free, and he's not to be clutched or held or pinned down by anybody ever again.
Narrator	They didn't say any more, but got up and dashed back to Jerusalem – all seven miles of it.
Cleopas	This is the place to be! This is where God's bringing new hope out of all that pain.
Narrator	And he was right.

Belonging to God's community

Ruth

Preparation page

What's the point?

The universality of God's love is graphically represented here. Ruth's selfless loyalty to Naomi generates a response not only in Naomi but in her relative, Boaz – and all this in the context of a historical antipathy between their different nations. This is particularly startling in the light of Deuteronomy 23:3: 'No Ammonite or Moabite shall be admitted to the Assembly of the Lord. Even to the tenth generation, none of their descendants shall be admitted to the assembly of the Lord.' (NRSV)

In Ruth, God's love broke down a monumental barrier: Ruth's great-grandson, David, was not only admitted to the assembly but became regarded as their greatest-ever king!

Preparation

Make a wedding canopy. This can be as simple or as elaborate as you like – for example, a sheet, decorated with paper cut-outs and attached to a broomstick at each corner. When Jewish couples marry, the couple traditionally stand under some kind of canopy to symbolise the home they will share. In the time of Ruth it would probably have been simply a prayer-shawl, held aloft by friends. You're going to do something a little different, though, and you'll need room for quite a number of people under your canopy, so you might decide to include a few extra poles and let more children share the job of holding it up.

Suggested songs

God made a boomerang
I'm black, I'm white
Let love be real
Seek ye first the kingdom of God
Lord, the light of your love is shining

Checklist

At the service you will need:

- the wedding canopy
- several willing volunteers to hold it up!

All-age worship

Opening song

A song praising and celebrating the faithfulness of God

Prayer

Loving God, we thank you that your love holds all creation together.
We thank you that you make no judgements about race or ancestry,
but love us all the same.
Please forgive us when we label people and treat them badly,
and help us to become signs of your love to everybody we encounter.
Through Jesus Christ our Lord.
Amen.

Word and action

Word: Ruth
Mixed marriage, mixed monarchy

(See page 97 for a dramatised version of this story.)

Now, I've got to ask it – just how much misfortune can one person take? I mean, take Naomi, for example. Everything had seemed fine when she moved from Israel to Moab with her husband and two little boys. Even when her husband died, she managed to look after her sons, and when they grew up they married two women from Moab called Ruth and Orpah, and things seemed to be good again. Then, the real disaster struck. Naomi's sons died, as well. So there she was, in a foreign country, with no one in the world but her two daughters-in-law. And the trouble was that in those days it was really hard for a woman to earn a living – all the good jobs were for men, but there weren't any men in Naomi's family any more.

Then Naomi heard that things were really good in Israel – there'd been a great harvest that year, and people had jobs and money again. 'Let's go back to Israel,' Naomi suggested.

On the way back, though, Naomi realised that it wasn't a case of 'back' to Israel for Ruth and Orpah – they were Moabites, and they were leaving their own country to be with her. 'Look,' she said, 'you stay in Moab – you're young, you're beautiful, and you'll have a good chance of marrying again. You're much better off here. Anyway, you know what my people can be like about Moabites – I hate to say it, but most of my people don't like yours at all. You'll have a rough time if you come with me.'

Orpah cried, kissed Naomi goodbye and turned back, but Ruth was determined. 'Look, here, Mum-in-law,' she said, 'I'm not giving up on you that easily – I'll go wherever you go. From now on, your people are my people, your God is my God – and may God do his worst to me if I let you down. Got it?'

So it was that they arrived in Israel together. 'Just think,' said Naomi, sadly, 'I left here a rich woman, and I'm coming back as poor as a synagogue spider. We've got to find a way of earning a living.'

'Let me worry about that,' Ruth said. 'I'll go and be a gleaner – it's not much but there's money to be earned picking up the corn the reapers drop. I'll do that.'

Now, what do you think happened? Well, it turned out that Ruth was working in a field owned by a rich relation of Naomi's. Boaz was his name, and he was impressed – seriously impressed. 'Who's that woman working in the field?' he asked his manager.

'Oh, just some Moabite,' replied the other. 'Ruth, a friend of Naomi. Tell you what – she's a good worker.'

Boaz went over to speak to Ruth. 'Stay in this field,' he said, 'and I'll make sure no one bothers you. And if you want a drink, just ask – now, what are you doing for lunch?'

So it was that Boaz and Ruth began to get to know each other – and it wasn't long before Naomi caught on. 'Boaz!' she exclaimed. 'He's a relation of mine – rich, and kind with it, and that's a combination you don't often find.'

Time went by, and Naomi decided she'd better give events a bit of help. 'Boaz will be working late tonight, and he'll probably sleep in the barn,' she told Ruth. 'Now go and get yourself dolled up – nothing obvious, mind, he doesn't go for that sort of woman – and just go and lie down near to him so that when he wakes up he finds you there. If he can't take a hint like that, then he's really got a problem!'

Boaz, naturally, was a perfect gentleman. 'You'd better slip out of here,' he said, 'before people get the wrong idea. Look, according to our laws, Naomi's *nearest* relative is supposed to provide for you – so I've got to give him the chance. If he doesn't want to, then the way's clear for us to be married. Let me talk to him first – with a bit of luck he'll give us his blessing.'

And that's how it happened that Ruth, a Moabite, a member of the race that most Israelites really hated, showed how love and kindness can break down even the worst bad feelings.

And that's not the end of the story. After they were married, Ruth became a mother . . . and then a grandmother . . . and then a great-grandmother. And who do you think her great-grandson was? A chap called David – remember him, the shepherd boy turned giant-killer, turned king of all Israel? And all because Ruth had cared about Naomi enough to stick with her!

Action

Get some of the children to hold the poles of the canopy.

Explain the significance of the canopy – a shared home where people live in a bond of love – and ask for volunteers to come and simply stand beneath the canopy representing the great variety of people in the church: male, female, old, young, people from other denominations or of different ethnic origins – try to get as much variety as possible. If people want to volunteer, and explain why they think their specific attributes are important ('I'm a senior citizen, and I bring a lot of experience with me'), then let them do so. Finally, simply point out to everyone – whether under the canopy or still in the pews – that this is a great visual aid of the world God wants: lots of different people all sharing the same world-home. You might also use the canopy as a symbol of the overarching love of God, under which we are all united and valued in our diversity.

Song 2

Offering

This may be introduced as our offering of ourselves, as well as our gifts, to God, that he may use us to show his love in the world.

Offertory prayer

Loving God, we offer you our gifts,
not just of money but the great variety of talents, skills, culture
that we each bring to your service.
Take all that we offer and use us as a sign of your love in the world.
Amen.

Song 3

Reading

1 John 4:7-11 read from a standard Bible. Introduce it with words such as: We've thought a lot about the nature and quality of God's love, as seen through his people. John reminds us that we have a gospel not of works but of grace.

Talk (optional)

If you feel it appropriate (and if time permits) reinforce the point made in the introduction to the reading. Christianity is primarily about what God does – not what we do. The reason we are to love one another unconditionally is not that God tells us to, but that God does it! This is how we are loved. This makes loving one another not an irksome duty but a joyful (and free!) response to what we have received.

Notices and family news

Prayers of intercession

Song 4

Closing prayer/benediction

Dramatised reading
Mixed marriage, mixed monarchy

Narrator	Now, I've got to ask it – just how much misfortune can one person take? I mean, take Naomi, for example. Everything had seemed fine when she moved from Israel to Moab with her husband and two little boys. Even when her husband died, she managed to look after her sons, and when they grew up they married two women from Moab, called Ruth and Orpah, and things seemed to be good again. Then, the real disaster struck. Naomi's sons died, as well. So there she was, in a foreign country, with no one in the world but her two daughters-in-law.
Naomi	And the trouble was that in those days it was really hard for a woman to earn a living – all the good jobs were for men, but there weren't any men in my family any more. What was I to do?
Narrator	Then Naomi heard that things were really good in Israel – there'd been a great harvest that year, and people had jobs and money again.
Naomi	Let's go back to Israel – all three of us.
Narrator	On the way back, though, Naomi realised that it wasn't a case of 'back' to Israel for Ruth and Orpah – they were Moabites, and they were leaving their own country to be with her.
Naomi	Look, you stay in Moab – you're young, you're beautiful, and you'll have a good chance of marrying again. You're much better off here. Anyway, you know what my people can be like about Moabites – I hate to say it, but most of my people don't like yours at all. You'll have a rough time if you come with me.
Narrator	Orpah cried, kissed Naomi goodbye and turned back, but Ruth was determined.
Ruth	Look, here, Mum-in-law. I'm not giving up on you that easily – I'll go wherever you go. From now on, your people are my people, your God is my God – and may God do his worst to me if I let you down. Got it?
Narrator	So it was that they arrived in Israel together.
Naomi	Just think. I left here a rich woman, and I'm coming back as poor as a synagogue spider. We've got to find a way of earning a living.
Ruth	Let me worry about that. I'll go and be a gleaner – it's not much but there's money to be earned picking up the corn the reapers drop. I'll do that.
Narrator	Now, what do you think happened? Well, it turned out that Ruth was working in a field owned by a rich relation of Naomi's. Boaz was his name, and he was impressed – seriously impressed. He called his farm manager over.
Boaz	Who's that woman working in the field?
Manager	Oh, just some Moabite – Ruth, a friend of Naomi.

Boaz	A *loyal* friend, from what I've heard.
Manager	Yes, and she's a good worker.
Boaz	You make sure she doesn't get any trouble for the men. OK?
Manager	As you say, sir.
Narrator	Boaz went over to speak to Ruth.
Boaz	Stay in this field, and I'll make sure no one bothers you. And if you want a drink, just ask – now, what are you doing for lunch?
Narrator	So it was that Boaz and Ruth began to get to know each other – and it wasn't long before Naomi caught on.
Naomi	Boaz? He's a relation of mine – rich, and kind with it, and that's a combination you don't often find. Look, he'll be working late tonight, and he'll probably sleep in the barn. Now, go and get yourself dolled up – nothing obvious, mind, he doesn't go for that sort of woman – and just go and lie down near to him so that when he wakes up he finds you there. If he can't take a hint like that, then he's really got a problem!
Narrator	So, when Boaz woke up the next morning, he could smell beautiful perfume.
Boaz	Well, either I'm starting a new trend in male fashions, or there's a woman here.
Narrator	And, of course, there was. And of course, it worked. Boaz, naturally, was a perfect gentleman.
Boaz	You'd better slip out of here, before people get the wrong idea. Look, according to our laws, Naomi's nearest relative is supposed to provide for you – so I've got to give him the chance. If he doesn't want to, then the way's clear for us to be married. Let me talk to him first – with a bit of luck he'll give us his blessing.
Narrator	And that's how it happened that Ruth, a Moabite, a member of the race that most Israelites really hated, showed how love and kindness can break down even the worst bad feelings.
Naomi	And that's not the end of the story. After they were married, Ruth became a mother . . . and then a grandmother . . . and then a great-grandmother. And who do you think her great-grandson was? A chap called David – remember him, the shepherd boy turned giant-killer, turned king of all Israel? And all because Ruth had cared enough to stick with me!

The feeding of the five thousand _____

Preparation page

What's the point?

In the eyes of contemporary adults, the child would have nothing to offer. In fact, he has more than anyone else. Apart from being the only one there with food, he has the generosity to share what little he has. Dr Pauline Cutting tells how, when in the besieged refugee camp in Beirut, she was struck by the generosity with which the Palestinian refugees shared their meagre food – food which they would then have to brave sniper fire to replace. Once, she protested, 'But you can't give to me – you have so little.' Her host replied, 'While I have a little, I will give you a little. When I have nothing, *then* I will give you nothing.'

It is a humbling fact of aid workers' experience that it is often among those with apparently least to offer that they find the most generous hospitality – and, by implication, the most powerful signs of God's love.

Preparation

Take seven large sheets of white paper – flip-chart pages would do nicely – and draw or paint a single fish on each of two of them and a single bread roll on each of the other five (the quality of the artwork isn't the most vital thing). This is obviously the ideal number, but don't be afraid to add or deduct sheets according to the usual size of your congregation. You should think in terms of having at least four and preferably not more than twelve people to each sheet. Ensure there is at least one bold marker pen available for each sheet.

Suggested songs

5 0 0 0 + hungry folk
A new commandment
Feed the hungry people

Checklist

At the service you will need:

* the flip-chart pages
* marker pens

All-age worship

Opening song

A song praising and celebrating the faithfulness of God

Prayer

Loving God, we're here both to give and to receive.
Help us in our worship to receive what each has to offer,
as well as being ready to give whatever we may.
Please forgive us for not always recognising and valuing each other's gifts,
and help us to share your love as we learn to do so.
Amen.

Word and action

Action

Tell the congregation you're going to have a theological picnic! Divide them into (preferably seven) groups (don't be afraid to vary that up or down if numbers dictate) and get the children to hand out the 'tablecloths'. There's not much food for each group, is there – just one roll or one small fish? Ask them to talk about what they feel they as a group can offer to the shared life of the church. Emphasise the importance of their identifying and affirming *each other's* particular contributions. It may be something like leading music, cleaning the church, gardening, or perhaps something more 'hidden' – their own private prayer for the church and its people. It may simply be their faithful attendance week by week. For each item, they can draw another loaf or fish – or perhaps a glass of wine or cup of tea! – on the sheet. After a little while, get someone from each group to come forward and show the rest of the church what kind of picnic they've been having.

Hopefully, each sheet will contain a lot more food than the single item that was on it to start with. Now they're going to hear a story about how Jesus took the small gift that a child was willing to share, and used it to work an amazing miracle.

Word: John 6:1-13
Help me feed the world

(See page 103 for a dramatised version of this story.)

I tell you, it was the most amazing thing of my life. I remember, I was about ten years old at the time, and everybody made me feel it. Young, that is. If it wasn't, 'You're too young to understand,' it was, 'Go and play while your mother and I talk about something important.' Not that I had bad parents mind you – that's how it was for kids in those days.

My mum explained it all to me. 'One day, Ben,' she said – that's my name, Ben – 'One day, Ben, you'll be grown-up, and you'll be important. But now – well, go and play somewhere, there's a good boy.' Sometimes, it made me hopping mad – I mean, I may be a kid but I'm not stupid. You know, I look around at the world the way the grown-ups have made it, and – well, if that's how clever they are, I'm not impressed. I mean, I'm seriously not impressed.

Then Jesus came to town – well, to the hills outside it, but that's near enough. Everyone was going to see him – everyone except my mum and dad who had something important to do, as usual. 'You can go, if you like,' Mum said. 'I'll pack you up a bit of lunch, and while you're away your dad and I can decide what colour to paint your bedroom. Yes, I know you want yellow walls, but we'll decide what's right for you.'

So that's how I came to be out in the hills, with a full sandwich box and an empty schedule, just waiting to see what Jesus would say. And a good thing too – if I hadn't been there, I don't know what would have happened. The place was absolutely crowded, and there seemed to be some kind of argument going on among Jesus' friends.

'Don't blame me, it's not my fault,' I heard Philip saying.

'I'm not blaming you, Phil,' Jesus answered. 'I'm just asking, that's all – where can we get some food for all these people?'

Well, I knew I didn't have much, but it would be a start, so I went up to one of the gang and said, 'You can have my lunch if you'd like it.'

One of them smiled very kindly – you know, the way grown-ups do when they're trying to humour you – and said, 'It's nice of you, sonny,' – don't you just hate being called names like that? – 'It's nice of you, sonny, but you leave this to us.'

Well, I'd had enough of that kind of thing from my parents, without getting it from complete strangers, too. I know it wasn't very polite, but I couldn't help saying, 'You got a better idea?'

'Look here, kid,' Philip interrupted, 'I know you mean well, but this is grown-ups' stuff, OK?'

'Please yourself,' I said, and was about to go away when Andrew came over. I'd met Andrew before, and he's not bad as grown-ups go.

'What've you got?' he asked. And he didn't sneer when he saw it. 'Hey, Jesus,' he called, 'there's a lad here with five bread rolls and a couple of fish – not much for all these people, but how about it?'

I couldn't believe it – Jesus seemed really glad I was there. 'Hey, you guys,' he called to his friends, 'take a look at this. Is this terrific, or is this terrific? Well, don't just stand there – tell everyone to sit down, and then start serving.'

I don't know how Jesus did it, but everyone was fed – and I had plenty myself, as well. And afterwards, when we'd all eaten, he told us to collect up the bits people had dropped, so they wouldn't go to waste. Twelve baskets, we filled – no kidding, twelve – so there was more left over when he'd finished than I'd given him in the beginning. Weird – I mean, really weird.

When I got home, I couldn't wait to tell my mum and dad. 'Hey, guess what?' I said. 'I just helped Jesus feed five thousand people.'

'That's nice, dear,' said Mum. 'I hope you didn't get in the way. Now go and tidy your room while I get some dinner.'

Grown-ups – I ask you! Tell you one thing: I bet Jesus wouldn't send me away when I'd got something interesting to tell him.

Song 2

Offering

This may be introduced as our way, first of recognising that all we have is God's gift to us, and then of showing our love in return.

Offertory prayer

Holy and loving God,
we thank you for all that you give to us.
Accept these gifts as a sign of our willingness to share.
Through Jesus Christ our Lord.
Amen.

Song 3

Reading

1 Corinthians 11:17-28 read from a standard Bible. Introduce it with words such as: Paul emphasises that it is the quality of the sharing which defines the Church as the Body of Christ.

Talk (optional)

If you feel it appropriate (and if time permits) you may like to say that what Paul is unhappy about here is the quality of the community, reflected in people's attitude to sharing. Selfish attitudes mean that the poorer people are being left out. The rich get there first and get more than their share, and others who are more needy don't get enough. So, for us, belonging to God's community means taking time to consider each other, and being willing to share.

Notices and family news

Prayers of intercession

Song 4

Closing prayer/benediction

Dramatised reading
Help me feed the world

Narrator   I tell you, it was the most amazing thing of my life. I remember, I was about ten years old at the time, and everybody made me feel it. Young, that is. If it wasn't, 'You're too young to understand,' it was, 'Go and play while your mother and I talk about something important.' Not that I had bad parents mind you – that's how it was for kids in those days. My mum explained it all to me.

Mother   One day, Ben, you'll be grown up, and you'll be important. But now – well, go and play somewhere, there's a good boy.

Narrator   Sometimes, it made me hopping mad – I mean, I may be a kid but I'm not stupid. You know, I look around at the world the way the grown-ups have made it, and – well, if that's how clever they are, I'm not impressed. I mean, I'm seriously not impressed. Then Jesus came to town – well, to the hills outside it, but that's near enough. Everyone was going to see him – everyone except my mum and dad who had something important to do, as usual.

Mum   You can go, if you like. I'll pack you up a bit of lunch, and while you're away your dad and I can decide what colour to paint your bedroom. Yes, I know you want yellow walls, but we'll decide what's right for you.

Narrator   So that's how I came to be out in the hills, with a full sandwich box and an empty schedule, just waiting to see what Jesus would say. And a good thing too – if I hadn't been there, I don't know what would have happened. The place was absolutely crowded, and there seemed to be some kind of argument going on among Jesus' friends.

Philip   Don't blame me, Jesus – it's not my fault.

Jesus   I'm not blaming you, Phil. I'm just asking, that's all – where can we get some food for all these people?

Narrator   Well, I knew I didn't have much, but it would be a start, so I went up and offered them my lunch. Philip smiled very kindly – you know, the way grown-ups do when they're trying to humour you.

Philip   It's nice of you, sonny ...

Narrator   Don't you just hate being called names like that?

Philip   It's nice of you, sonny, but I you leave this to us.

Narrator   Well, I'd had enough of that kind of thing from my parents, without getting it from complete strangers, too. I know it wasn't very polite, but I couldn't help myself. [*To Philip*] You got a better idea?

Philip   Look here, kid, I know you mean well, but this is grown-ups' stuff, OK?

Narrator   Please yourself. [*To congregation*] I was about to go away when Andrew came over. I'd met Andrew before, and he's not bad as grown-ups go.

Andrew	What've you got?
Narrator	I thought he'd probably just laugh at my few rolls and fish, but he didn't.
Andrew	Hey, Jesus, there's a lad here with five bread rolls and a couple of fish – not much for all these people, but how about it?
Narrator	I couldn't believe it – Jesus seemed really glad I was there.
Jesus	Hey, you guys, take a look at this. Is this terrific, or is this terrific? Well, don't just stand there – tell everyone to sit down, and then start serving.
Narrator	I don't know how Jesus did it, but everyone was fed – and I had plenty myself, as well. And afterwards, when we'd all eaten, he told us to collect up the bits people had dropped, so they wouldn't go to waste. Twelve baskets, we filled – no kidding, twelve – so there was more left over when he'd finished than I'd given him in the beginning. Weird – I mean, really weird. When I got home, I couldn't wait to tell my mum and dad.
Narrator	Hey, guess what? I just helped Jesus feed five thousand people.
Mum	That's nice, dear. I hope you didn't get in the way. Now go and tidy your room while I get some dinner.
Narrator	Grown-ups – I ask you! Tell you one thing: I bet Jesus wouldn't send me away when I'd got something interesting to tell him.

The wedding at Cana

Preparation page

What's the point?

It wasn't at just any old party that Jesus worked this miracle, but at a wedding – a celebration of relationship. Here is his 'sign' that the new life God offers is supposed to be enjoyable, not in a selfish way, but in the giving of ourselves to one another. It's about belonging!

Preparation

Join several flip-chart sheets together to make a really big piece of paper (just bearing in mind that you'll need room to display it in the worship area!) and paint a picture of a large sparkling-wine bottle with a fountain of wine spurting from the top. (See 'Action' in the All-age service for how this would be used.) On the label, you could write 'Chateau X 2002' – 'X' being the name of your village or suburb; change the year as appropriate. Then draw some droplet shapes (large enough to write a few words on each) on white or buff card, and cut them out – enough for everyone in the church to have one.

Suggested songs

Come on and celebrate
Jesus turned the water into wine
Let's sing and make music to the Lord
Oh! Oh! Oh! How good is the Lord
The time has come to have some fun

Checklist

At the service you will need:

- the large picture already on display
- the 'droplet' cards to be given out with the hymn books
- some pens or pencils for the congregation
- Blu-Tack or pins

All-age worship

Opening song

A song praising and celebrating the faithfulness of God

Prayer

Loving God, thank you for showing us in Jesus that you love life,
and want it to be celebrated.
Help us to join in that by the way we give ourselves to each other,
and share our lives together.
Forgive us when our commitment falls so far short,
and help us to grow into a community that is a sign of your love.
Through Jesus Christ our Lord.
Amen.

Word and action

Word: John 2:1-11
Chateau heaven '27

(See page 109 for a dramatised version of this story.)

Can you imagine having a party and running out of food, because your parents hadn't provided enough? I mean, would that be embarrassing, or would that be embarrassing? Well, that's probably how Tom and Becky felt at their wedding, when the wine ran out.

'Someone didn't order enough of it,' Tom said angrily.

'Oh, that's right,' Becky answered, 'find someone to blame, just as long as it isn't you.'

'Now, now, you two,' came a friendly voice, 'try not to have a row at your own wedding – you've got a whole lifetime for that sort of thing. Now, let's see what can be done about it before everybody notices and it all gets ugly.'

The voice belonged to Mary, and she turned to her son who was there with some of his friends – right in the middle of an interesting conversation.

'Oh, come off it, Jesus,' Simon was saying, 'If Sumarcus hadn't made an unscheduled pit stop, he'd have won that chariot race by a lap.'

'Right, Jesus, my lad,' Mary interrupted, briskly, 'time to make yourself useful – they've run out of wine.'

'Oh, really, Mother!' Jesus answered. 'Since when were you and I in the catering business? Look, I don't want to get into all that stuff yet – it's not time.'

Mary gave her son an old-fashioned look – the kind that only a Jewish mother can give to her son – before she turned to a couple of waiters standing nearby, and said, 'Just do whatever he tells you – OK? He's a good boy, underneath it all – he won't let you down.'

Now, standing near the door were some big water tubs. And I mean big – around, oh, 20 gallons, maybe 30, in each. They were used for washing guests' feet when they arrived, and, yes, I know it's a rather strange way of saying, 'How nice of you to come,' but when everyone wears open sandals and the roads are made of pure dust, well, it's the polite thing to do – or at least it was then. Jesus looked across at the water containers and said, 'Oh, I think they'll do.'

Tom wasn't exactly happy, and Becky was rapidly losing what was left of her cool. 'You give that to my guests to drink,' she said to Jesus, 'and I'll never speak to you again.' Then she turned to Tom, 'But you won't get off so lightly – I'll have a few things to say to you.'

Oh, dear! Now, you or I might have been a bit fazed by that – but not Jesus. 'Top up the jars,' he told the waiters, 'fill them right to the brim.'

The waiters looked at one another in disbelief, but they did as they were told – arguing with Jesus would have been one thing, but his mother was quite another proposition. 'Now, pour some of it out and take it to the caterer to taste,' Jesus said.

The waiters' hands were shaking as they lifted the heavy jars between them and began to pour the water into a jug. But, hang on a minute – what was happening? The water was a very funny colour. Nothing strange in that, of course – people weren't that fussy about what kind of water they used for washing guests' feet – but this water wasn't dirty; it was a rich, deep-red colour. The waiters were amazed, and went to take some to the caterer to taste.

'That's my boy, Jesus,' Mary beamed. 'I knew you wouldn't let me down.'

Becky still wasn't happy, though. 'Look,' she said, 'anyone can play tricks with a bit of food colouring – you just wait until the caterer tastes it. Oh, it's going to be so embarrassing.'

They turned to see the waiter pouring some of the liquid into a cup for the caterer to try. 'Any moment now . . .' said Becky. The caterer sniffed at the cup. Becky saw his lips move. 'He hates it!' she shouted at Tom. 'I knew it – you've embarrassed me in front of all your friends. I'll never speak to you again – you're pathetic!'

The caterer's face broke into a big smile of approval before he finished off the cup, and the waiters started serving it to the guests. One of them went over to Tom. 'He's well pleased,' he told him. 'Most weddings we do, they use the best wine first – then when everyone's too plastered to notice, they serve up the rubbish. He reckons you've saved the best of the wine until the end.'

Becky squealed with delight, and threw her arms around Tom's neck. 'Darling!' she gushed. 'I never doubted you for a minute!'

Mary gave Jesus a proud smile that seemed to say, 'That's my lovely boy,' but fortunately Jesus didn't notice. He was back to his conversation with Simon.

'I'll say this for you, Jesus,' Simon said. 'You may not have a clue about chariot racing, but you certainly know your wine.'

Action

Ask the congregation to spend a few moments in discussion groups. You want them to identify the good things in your local community that you can help people to enjoy more, and write them on their cards. Also, think about who gets left out when there isn't enough to go round. For example, good local shops might be little use to a housebound person who can't get there, so part of sharing God's new wine might be in providing transport. Or perhaps the church has really good premises that could be used for community activities, or a car park not in use six days a week where a fair-trade market could be set up.

Those are just a few ideas, but no doubt the groups will think of more and better ones from their local knowledge. After a few minutes, ask the groups to share their ideas, and let the children Blu-Tack the droplets on to the picture so you have a shower of God's goodness gushing out of the wine bottle! Then put the contents of the cards on to your meeting agendas and get the church to act on them!

Song 2

Offering

This may be introduced as symbolic of the sharing of life – its downs as well as its ups – that is at the heart of being church.

Offertory prayer

Thank you, Lord God, for all you offer to us,
without asking whether we deserve it or not.
Accept what we are able to offer in return,
as a sign of our commitment to sharing your love both here and beyond.
Amen.

Song 3

Reading

Acts 2:44-47 read from a standard Bible. Introduce it with words such as: The feast, of course, is but a symbol of an entire lifestyle, and Scripture tells us how that was lived out in the early Church.

Talk (optional)

If you feel it appropriate (and if time permits) you may say that, while we might believe (not everyone does, of course!) that to take this reading literally is not appropriate in our context, we still need to ask ourselves what such an example actually does say about our life as a Christian community.

Notices and family news

Prayers of intercession

Song 4

Closing prayer/benediction

Dramatised reading
Chateau heaven '27

Narrator	Can you imagine having a party and running out of food, because your parents hadn't provided enough? I mean, would that be embarrassing, or would that be embarrassing? Well, that's probably how Tom and Becky felt at their wedding, when the wine ran out.
Tom	Someone didn't order enough of it, Becky.
Becky	Oh, that's right, Tom – find someone to blame, just as long as it isn't you.
Mary	Now, now, you two, try not to have a row at your own wedding – you've got a whole lifetime for that sort of thing. Now, let's see what can be done about it before everybody notices and it all gets ugly.
Narrator	Mary turned to her son who was there with some of his friends – right in the middle of an interesting conversation with Simon.
Simon	Oh, come off it, Jesus! If Sumarcus hadn't made an unscheduled pit stop, he'd have won that chariot race by a lap.
Mary	Right, Jesus, my lad, time to make yourself useful – they've run out of wine.
Jesus	Oh, really, Mother! Since when were you and I in the catering business? Look, I don't want to get into all that stuff yet – it's not time.
Narrator	Mary gave her son an old-fashioned look – the kind that only a Jewish mother can give to her son – before she turned to a couple of waiters standing nearby.
Mary	Just do whatever he tells you – OK? He's a good boy, underneath it all – he won't let you down.
Narrator	Now, standing near the door were some big water tubs. And I mean big – around, oh, 20 gallons, maybe 30, in each. They were used for washing guests' feet when they arrived, and, yes, I know it's a rather strange way of saying, 'How nice of you to come,' but when everyone wears open sandals and the roads are made of pure dust, well, it's the polite thing to do – or at least it was then. Jesus looked across at the water containers.
Jesus	Oh, I think they'll do.
Narrator	Tom wasn't exactly happy, and Becky was rapidly losing what was left of her cool.
Becky	You give that to my guests to drink, Jesus, and I'll never speak to you again. But *you* won't get off so lightly, Tom – I'll have a few things to say to you.
Narrator	Oh, dear! Now, you or I might have been a bit fazed by that – but not Jesus. He turned to give instructions to the waiters.
Jesus	Top up the jars. Fill them right to the brim.

Narrator	The waiters looked at one another in disbelief, but they did as they were told – arguing with Jesus would have been one thing, but his mother was quite another proposition.
Jesus	Now, pour some of it out and take it to the caterer to taste.
Narrator	The waiters' hands were shaking as they lifted the heavy jars between them and began to pour the water into a jug.
Waiter	Hang on a minute – what's happening? This water's a very funny colour.
Narrator	Nothing strange in that, of course – people weren't that fussy what kind of water they used for washing guests' feet – but this water wasn't dirty; it was a rich, deep-red colour. The waiters were amazed, and went to take some to the caterer to taste.
Mary	That's my boy, Jesus! I knew you wouldn't let me down.
Becky	Look, anyone can play tricks with a bit of food colouring – you just wait until the caterer tastes it. Oh, it's going to be *so* embarrassing.
Narrator	They turned to see the waiter pouring some of the liquid into a cup for the caterer to try.
Becky	Any moment now . . .
Narrator	The caterer sniffed at the cup. He took a sip of the wine, and his face broke into a big smile of approval before he finished off the cup and the waiters started serving it to the guests. One of them went over to Tom.
Waiter	He's well pleased. Most weddings we do, they use the best wine first – then when everyone's too plastered to notice, they serve up the rubbish. He reckons you've saved the best of the wine until the end.
Becky	Tom, darling! I never doubted you for a minute!
Narrator	Mary gave Jesus a proud smile that seemed to say, 'That's my lovely boy,' but fortunately Jesus didn't notice. He was back to his conversation with Simon.
Simon	I'll say this for you, Jesus, you may not have a clue about chariot racing, but you certainly know your wine.

The law and the prophets

Moses and the ten commandments

Preparation page

What's the point?

Freedom isn't the same as anarchy – none of us can be truly free if we don't feel safe. We need structure, and a basic framework for living. So God's law is intended to set us free – not make us into slaves again!

Preparation

Make something to represent a prison cell. This could be as simple as a barred window cut from cardboard, for the prisoner to hold in front of his or her face, or you could beg some large cardboard boxes from a removal company and use these to make a complete cell – or go for various stages in-between. Now, you need a volunteer to go into the cell during the service and refuse to come out because they don't trust the congregation – if they want to give one or two reasons, such as 'They don't like City supporters', that's fine, but keep it light-hearted.

Suggested songs

A new commandment
Jesus, reign in me
Lord, the light of your love is shining
Obey the maker's instructions

Checklist

At the service you will need:
- the 'cell', ready for use
- a volunteer to be in the cell
- a flip chart or board and pens or chalk

All-age worship

Opening song

A song praising and celebrating the faithfulness of God

Prayer

Loving God, thank you for showing us in Jesus
that you're always with us in any circumstances,
offering both hope and challenge from within the situation.
Thank you for showing us in Moses
that that is how you have always liked to work.
So, be within this service –
call us, challenge us and fill us with your hope;
forgive us for our pessimism and lack of trust,
and help us live as your people in our day-to-day lives.
Amen.

Word and action

Action

Get the volunteer into the cell or behind the barred window (you may find it best for them to be in position before the service starts) and ask them why they're there. Why have they locked themselves away from the congregation? How much you hype this up will depend on your congregation and the acting ability of the 'prisoner' – the important thing to make clear is that the person doesn't feel safe outside the cell.

Now, get the congregation talking about how they can help people not to feel afraid – bearing in mind that many people outside the church find it very difficult to cross the threshold. What kinds of rules can you put in place to help people feel safe?

Examples might include not looking down on people who dress shabbily, not discriminating against people on racial grounds (or on the grounds of the football team they support!). It should go without saying, but not gossiping about people might be a good one.

This activity could be done either in groups or with the whole congregation together. Whichever you do, write up the rules they come up with. Then turn to the person in the cell and ask them if they feel safe to come out now. (It may be best if it's pre-arranged that they will say 'yes' to this question!) Then, when they have rejoined the congregation, you can simply point out that rules aren't supposed to be a burden – we all need some kind of structure before we can enjoy our freedom! In the exercise you've just done, it was the lack of rules that caused the person to be locked up – good ground rules enabled them to be free! The purpose of God's law was to provide a safe place where people could enjoy freedom.

Now, have the story read in either narrative or dramatised form.

Word: Exodus 18:13-20:17

Rules for free people

(See page 118 for a dramatised version of this story.)

OK, the Israelites have left Egypt, so they're not slaves any more, and they're on their way to the land God's promised them. Moses is the one God's chosen to lead them – and what do you think he's spending all his time doing? Settling arguments – that's what. They just can't stop wrangling among themselves, and then Moses has to sort it out. His father-in-law, Jethro, notices. 'Hey, what's going on?' he says. 'Why are you spending your time settling quarrels – with long queues of people waiting around all day to see you when they should have work to do?'

'Someone's got to,' says Moses. 'When they have a quarrel, I tell them who's right.'

Jethro thinks Moses is doing it the hard way, and tells him so. 'You need help,' he says. 'Why not appoint judges to do this for you? You can tell everyone what God's rules are, and then the judges will be able to decide who's right and who's wrong. Of course, they can still bring the really difficult arguments to you, but you won't be worn out, and they'll get sorted.'

Well, that sounds good to Moses, so he does it – appoints lots of judges to settle people's arguments. But, hang on a minute – if you've got judges, you need laws, don't you?

Now, as it happens, the Israelites are camped near a big mountain, called Mount Sinai – so Moses hoofs it up the mountain to get a bit of peace and quiet and listen to God.

It's really spooky. Thick clouds and smoke – because God's chosen to show himself to Moses in fire.* So it's dark, hot, and no place to be if you've got asthma.

'This is our place,' God says to Moses. 'Yours and mine. The rest of the people can wait expectantly at the bottom of the hill. *Are* the people waiting expectantly?'

'Oh, yes, Lord,' Moses assures him. 'They're all waiting. Expectantly.'

'Then you'd better go back down and make sure they don't get any big ideas and start to follow you,' God tells him. 'And while you're down there, you can fetch your brother Aaron and bring him up here to me.'

So, Moses has to go all the way back down, give them the message, and then bring Aaron back up the mountain. Then God lays down the law. 'I'm God,' he says, 'and don't you forget it. Remember *I* set you free, and don't go worshipping other gods, because it won't do you any good. OK?'

'OK, God, you're the boss,' Moses and Aaron say.

'Good,' says God. 'And I don't want you making statues to worship, either. Oh, yes, I know it goes on, but I'm too great to be represented by a statue – or a picture, come to that – so it's me you're going to worship. And another thing. Don't use my name in bad ways.'

---

* Can the children think of another time when God showed himself to Moses in fire? It's not in this book, but some of them may know.

Moses and Aaron aren't too sure what that means. 'You mean, like using it as a swear word?'

'Yes, and other things, too.' God tells them. 'Anyway, moving on: have a special day for rest and worship – a holy day when you can listen to me, and think about other things that are really important – and yes, I know you do that every day, but once a week you can make a point of it. Got it?'

'Oh, yes, God,' Moses and Aaron say, 'we've got it.'

'Good,' God says. 'Now, that's about you and me. I've got some more rules, and they're about you and each other. And it all starts with respect – respect your parents, because that's your first step to long life and happiness in the new land I'm giving you. And respect for others is what it's all about really – like, if you respect people, you won't kill them, will you? Husbands and wives won't cheat on one another, and you won't take things that don't belong to you – no, not even to borrow, unless you ask first.'

Aaron looks a bit embarrassed at this. 'You know that hammer you lost, Moses? Well, I'll give it back to you when we get home.'

'Moving quickly on,' God continues, 'just a couple more. Don't tell lies about people. And don't come that "sticks and stones" rubbish with me, either. Words *do* hurt – and gossip ruins lives. So don't do it. OK?'

'OK, God – you're the boss.'

'Now,' says God, 'if you want to be really safe, "Don't do it" isn't enough. It's "Don't even think about it". Don't even *think* about wanting things other people have got – whether it's gismos, gadgets, goats or girlfriends. And the same goes for boyfriends, too. Now, tell the people to keep those ten rules and they won't go far wrong.'

'Oh, yes,' says Aaron. 'We'll all keep them all the time,'

Well, if they had they might have got on a little better. But we all know how hard keeping the rules can be, don't we?

Song 2

Offering

This may be introduced as a token of the obedience we offer to God, not fearfully or reluctantly, but joyfully and freely, to enable his true freedom to be enjoyed by others.

Offertory prayer

Loving God, you have made us to be free,
and invited us freely to share in your creative work.
So here, in trust and obedience to your call,
we gladly offer you ourselves and our gifts,
that the world may know your love.
Amen.

Song 3

Reading

Matthew 22:35-40 read from a standard Bible. Introduce it with words such as: Jesus gives us in very few words a summary of the essence of God's law – the heart of the commandments given to Moses and all the mass of laws that flowed from them – in a couple of sentences.

Talk (optional)

If you feel it appropriate (and if time permits) you might point out that Moses, the lawgiver, was also the person God chose to set the people free – no mere coincidence! So the ethical content of our faith is neither to be harshly imposed, damaging people's lives, nor lightly ignored as though it doesn't matter. Acting in truly loving ways is the heart of it.

Notices and family news

Prayers of intercession

Song 4

Closing prayer/benediction

Dramatised reading
Rules for free people

Narrator	OK, the Israelites have left Egypt, so they're not slaves any more, and they're on their way to the land God's promised them. Moses is the one God's chosen to lead them – and what d'you think he's spending all his time doing? Settling arguments, that's what. They just can't stop wrangling among themselves, and then Moses has to sort it out. His father-in-law, Jethro, notices.
Jethro	Hey, what's going on, Moses? Why are you spending your time settling quarrels – with long queues of people waiting around all day to see you, when they should have work to do?
Moses	Someone's got to. When they have a quarrel, I tell them who's right.
Jethro	You need help. Why not appoint judges to do this for you? You can tell everyone what God's rules are, and then the judges will be able to decide who's right and who's wrong. Of course, they can still bring the really difficult arguments to you, but you won't be worn out, and they'll get sorted.
Narrator	Well, that sounds good to Moses, so he does it – appoints lots of judges to settle people's arguments. But, hang on a minute – if you've got judges, you need laws, don't you? Now, as it happens, the Israelites are camped near a big mountain, called Mount Sinai – so Moses hoofs it up the mountain to get a bit of peace and quiet and listen to God. It's really spooky. Thick clouds and smoke – because God's chosen to show himself to Moses in fire. So it's dark, hot, and no place to be if you've got asthma. But God hasn't – so he can talk freely.
God	This is our place, Moses. Yours and mine. The rest of the people can wait expectantly at the bottom of the hill. *Are* the people waiting expectantly?
Moses	Oh, yes, Lord. They're all waiting. Expectantly.
God	Then you'd better go back down and make sure they don't get any big ideas and start to follow you. And while you're down there, you can fetch your brother Aaron and bring him up here to me.
Narrator	So, Moses has to go all the way back down, give them the message, and then bring Aaron back up the mountain. Then God lays down the law.
God	I'm God, and don't you forget it. Remember *I* set you free, and don't go worshipping other gods, because it won't do you any good. OK?
Moses	OK, God.
Aaron	You're the boss.
God	Good. And I don't want you making statues to worship, either. Oh, yes, I know it goes on, but I'm too great to be represented

by a statue – or a picture, come to that – so it's me you're going to worship. And another thing. Don't use my name in bad ways.

Moses Like, how, exactly?

Aaron You mean, like using it as a swear word?

God Yes, and other things, too. Anyway, moving on: have a special day for rest and worship – a holy day when you can listen to me, and think about other things that are really important – and yes, I know you do that every day, but once a week you can make a point of it. Got it?

Moses Oh, yes, God.

Aaron We've got it.

God Good. Now, that's about you and me. I've got some more rules, and they're about you and each other. And it all starts with respect – respect your parents, because that's your first step to long life and happiness in the new land I'm giving you. And respect for others is what it's all about really – like, if you respect people, you won't kill them, will you? Husbands and wives won't cheat on one another, and you won't take things that don't belong to you – no, not even to borrow, unless you ask first.

Aaron You know that hammer you lost, Moses? Well, I'll give it back to you when we get home.

God Moving quickly on, just a couple more. Don't tell lies about people. And don't come that 'sticks and stones' rubbish with me, either. Words *do* hurt – and gossip ruins lives. So don't do it. OK? And finally, if you want to be really safe, 'Don't do it' isn't enough. It's 'Don't even think about it'. Don't even think about wanting things other people have got – whether it's gismos, gadgets, goats or girlfriends. And, girls, the same goes for boyfriends, too. Now, tell the people to keep those ten rules and they won't go far wrong.

Elijah and the widow of Zarephath _____

Preparation page

What's the point?

Being a prophet is about a lot more than just foretelling the future. It begins with a really close relationship with God that allows someone to be a means whereby God can show his love to others.

Preparation

On a flip-chart pad, or other large sheet of paper, draw the outline of a jar that could be used for storing flour. (See 'Action' in the All-age worship for how this would be used.) You'll need to enclose most of the sheet within the outline to give plenty of space to write inside the 'jar'.

Suggested songs

I walk by faith
Jehovah Jireh, God will provide
Take my hands, Lord
When I needed a neighbour

Checklist

At the service, you will need:
- the flip chart with the drawing, already set up
- marker pens

All-age worship

Opening song

A song praising and celebrating the faithfulness of God

Prayer

Loving God,
thank you for your prophets who show your love to us.
Thank you for putting us in a world with other people –
for giving us one another to help and to be helped.
Please forgive us when we fail to notice what others have to offer,
or what we should be offering to them,
and help us to be like prophets ourselves
in showing your love to the world.
Amen.

Word and action

Word: 1 Kings 17:8-24
Prophet and loss

(See page 125 for a dramatised version of this story.)

Can you imagine having just enough food for one last meal – and knowing that after that you're going to starve to death? I can't – most of us will probably never know what that feels like – but let me introduce you to two people who know exactly how it feels.

Imagine the scene. Close your eyes, and we're going back in time – back, back, to before anyone we know was born . . . back to the time when Jesus was born, but we're not stopping; back even further to – oh, there's King Solomon building the temple – we've gone too far. Forward a bit: that's it – about, oh, eight or nine hundred years before Jesus was born. We're a little way off from the place that happened, too – in Zarephath, which is actually outside Israel, to the north of Galilee. It's really hot – I mean, so hot that nothing will grow. And a widow called Anna and her son Joe are going to have that last meal I mentioned.

So, there's Anna, out gathering sticks for firewood, when she sees this weird-looking guy. He's sitting on the ground to take the weight off his blistered feet, and his clothes look as though he's hiked across a desert in them – probably because he has. 'Excuse me, missus,' he says to her, 'but I could really murder a drink. Got a bit of water, have you?'

Now, remember, there's been no rain for yonks, so water's like gold – well, better, actually: what use is gold when you're thirsty? Still, Anna thinks, they're going to die anyway, so why not help this poor old man?

'Yes, OK – I'll go and get you some,' she says. Then as she walks away, she can't believe her ears.

'A nice bit of bread,' the man calls out. 'That'd be really cool.'

Anna turns round. 'Bread?' She repeats, incredulously. 'Bread! Look, mister, I've got just enough flour left to mix with about three drops of olive oil that's left in the jar, and I'm going to make a last meal for Joe and me – Joe's my boy – and then we're going to die of starvation. Give you bread? I think not, somehow.'

'Right,' says the man, 'I'll tell you what. I'm a prophet, see – a holy man – anyway, me and God, we're sort of close, you know. And he's promising that if you do this thing for me, your flour jar will never run out, and there'll always be olive oil in the bottle. So, how about it?'

Well, I ask you – here's this guy with his clothes in tatters and his feet growing fungus, who's obviously forgotten what water feels like on the skin, telling her he's God's agent and this is her big break. Would you believe him?

No, neither would I – but, for some reason, Anna *does* believe him – and the next thing she knows she's making this bread from the flour and oil and sitting down to eat it with her son, Joe, and – oh, did I tell you the prophet's name was Elijah? Well, that's put that right now, hasn't it.

But, you know, it's amazing. From that moment on, every time Anna goes to look for flour, she finds some in the jar. And every time she uses that last drop of olive oil from the bottle, some more appears. 'This is unbelievable!' she says. 'You're obviously a good sort to have around.'

Well, things go on OK for a while, but then Joe gets ill. I mean, really ill – like I hope you've never been – probably the heat and the water shortage that did it, but no one really knows. Anyway, nothing they do can save him, and he dies. 'Oh, I get it!' Anna screams at Elijah. 'This is what comes of having a holy man under my roof – you've reminded God of something I did wrong and he's punishing me for it by killing my child.' Well, don't be too hard on her – there are still people around even today who think that God does that kind of thing.

Anyway, Elijah doesn't argue – just says, 'Give the boy to me,' and takes him and puts him on his own bed. Then he prays like he's never prayed before. 'Hey, God, what's the story? I mean, just what d'you think you're doing? This woman's been really kind to me, and you go and do a horrible thing like this to her?' Then he prays, 'O God, give the lad his life back!' Nothing happens, so he says it again. Still nothing. Three times, he has to say it – three! – and suddenly, Joe starts breathing again. So Elijah gets him off the bed and straight downstairs to his mother. 'Hey,' he says, 'have I got news for you – here he is!'

Well, if Anna thought the flour and the oil were spectacular, she's got to be *seriously* impressed by this! 'No doubt about it,' she says, 'you're a man of God all right – I mean, why God should want to speak through someone with your dress sense, I don't really know – but he obviously does.'

Action

Have the story read, in either narrative or dramatised form, and then point out the picture on the flip chart. Just as God brought Elijah and the widow together to support each other, so he's done with this congregation. So you're now going to fill the flour jar with the great gifts God has given you in each other. These could include practical skills in cooking, carpentry or drain-clearing, artistic talents that can raise people's spirits or enliven worship, wonderful memories that the older people can use to entertain the younger – no doubt many things special to your church that writers of worship books would never think of.

As they're mentioned, write them up, starting at the bottom, and see if you can fill the flour jar. Here is God's provision for his people, given to them in one another!

Song 2

Offering

This may be introduced as symbolic of our willingness to offer ourselves as prophetic signs of God's love in the world.

Offertory prayer

Holy God, accept the gifts we bring,
both of our possessions and of ourselves,
and so perfect them
that we may be visible signs of your love in the world.
Amen.

Song 3

Reading

1 Corinthians 13 read from a standard Bible. Introduce it with words such as: St Paul places prophecy, along with all God's gifts, in the vital context of his love, which is at the heart of everything.

Talk (optional)

If you feel it appropriate (and if time permits) you can point out that the prophets weren't just about foretelling the future. That was only part of their role. They were reminders to the people of what it meant to be loved by God, and the responsibilities that involves for us in living as loved and loving people. For Elijah that meant both practical caring, as with widow of Zarephath, and denunciation of all that was unloving – which was how he came to be always upsetting Queen Jezebel!

Notices and family news

Prayers of intercession

Song 4

Closing prayer/benediction

Dramatised reading
Prophet and loss

Narrator	Can you imagine having just enough food for one last meal – and knowing that after that you're going to starve to death? I can't – most of us will probably never know what that feels like – but let me introduce you to two people who know exactly how it feels. Imagine the scene. Close your eyes, and we're going back in time – back, back, to before anyone we know was born . . . back to the time when Jesus was born, but we're not stopping; back even further to – oh, there's King Solomon building the temple – we've gone too far. Forward a bit: that's it – about, oh, eight or nine hundred years before Jesus was born. We're a little way off from the place that happened, too – in Zarephath, which is actually outside Israel, to the north of Galilee. It's really hot – I mean, so hot that nothing will grow. And a widow called Anna and her son Joe are going to have that last meal I mentioned – oh, you can open your eyes now, by the way. So, there's Anna, out gathering sticks for firewood when she sees this weird-looking guy. He's sitting on the ground to take the weight off his blistered feet, and his clothes look as though he's hiked across a desert in them – probably because he has.
Elijah	Excuse me, missus, but I could really murder a drink. Got a bit of water, have you?
Narrator	Now, remember, there's been no rain for yonks, so water's like gold – well, better, actually: what use is gold when you're thirsty? Still, Anna thinks, they're going to die anyway, so why not help this poor old man?
Anna	Yes, OK – I'll go and get you some.
Narrator	Then as she walks away, she can't believe her ears.
Elijah	A nice bit of bread. That'd be really cool.
Anna	Bread? Bread! Look, mister, I've got just enough flour left to mix with about three drops of olive oil that's left in the bottle, and I'm going to make a last meal for Joe and me – Joe's my boy – and then we're going to die of starvation. Give you bread? I think not, somehow.
Elijah	Right, I'll tell you what. I'm a prophet, see – my name's Elijah – anyway, me and God, we're sort of close, you know. And he's promising that if you do this thing for me your flour jar will never run out, and there'll always be olive oil in the bottle until the end of the water shortage. So, how about it?
Narrator	Well, I ask you – here's this guy with his clothes in tatters and his feet growing fungus, who's obviously forgotten what water feels like on the skin, telling her he's God's agent and this is her big break. Would you believe him? No, neither would I – but, for some reason, Anna *does* believe him – and the next thing she knows she's making this bread from the flour and oil

125

and sitting down to eat it with her son, Joe, and Elijah. But, you know, it's amazing. From that moment on, every time Anna goes to look for flour, she finds some in the jar. And every time she uses that last drop of olive oil from the bottle, some more appears.

Anna   This is unbelievable! You're obviously a good sort to have around.

Narrator   Well, things go on OK for a while, but then Joe gets ill. I mean, really ill – like I hope you've never been – probably the heat and the water shortage that did it, but no one really knows. Anyway, nothing they do can save him, and he dies. Anna really yells at Elijah.

Anna   Oh, I get it! This is what comes of having a holy man under my roof – you've reminded God of something I did wrong and he's punishing me for it by killing my child.

Narrator   Well, don't be too hard on her – there are still people around even today who think that God does that kind of thing.

Elijah   Give the boy to me.

Narrator   Elijah takes Joe and puts him on his own bed. Then he prays like he's never prayed before.

Elijah   Hey, God, what's the story? I mean, just what d'you think you're doing? This woman's been really kind to me, and you go and do a horrible thing like this to her? O God, give the lad his life back!

Narrator   Nothing happens, so he says it again. Still nothing. Three times, he has to say it – three! – and suddenly, Joe starts breathing again. So Elijah gets him off the bed and straight downstairs to his mother.

Elijah   Hey, have I got news for you – here he is!

Narrator   Well, if Anna thought the flour and the oil were spectacular, she's got to be *seriously* impressed by this!

Anna   No doubt about it, you're a man of God all right – I mean, why God should want to speak through someone with your dress sense, I don't really know – but he obviously does.

Jesus and the Transfiguration

Preparation page

What's the point?

Being seen by his disciples in the company of Moses and Elijah should have made the point that Jesus wasn't throwing out all their traditions but bringing them to fulfilment. The law and the prophets, traditionally represented by Moses and Elijah respectively, were ways God had shown his love for his people – and Jesus was going to raise that revelation to new heights.

Preparation

On a flip-chart pad, either draw a figure of Christ or, if you prefer, a cross to represent his presence. You might also want to prepare some cards – about postcard size – that can be Blu-Tacked around the picture during the service. Alternatively, you might prefer simply to write things up with a marker pen.

Suggested songs

Jesus is the lighthouse
Jesus' love is very wonderful
Lord, the light of your love is shining
Majesty

Checklist

At the service, you will need:

- the picture of Christ or a cross
- cards and/or marker pens
- some pens or pencils for the congregation
- Blu-Tack or pins

All-age worship

Opening song

A song praising and celebrating the faithfulness of God

Prayer

Loving God,
we thank you for all that has brought us here together –
all the journeys of faith that we've made,
the traditions we've come from,
the ideas and beliefs that have become important to us.
Most of all, though, we thank you for meeting us in your Son Jesus Christ,
and drawing us together into a living community.
Please forgive us when we lost sight of the living Christ
within our ideas and traditions,
and help us to rediscover the joy of being in his presence.
Amen.

Word and action

Action

Ask the congregation to spend a few minutes in groups identifying the different Christian traditions that are vital to their faith. For some people, perhaps, it might be scripture or prayer, some might say believers' baptism (others, equally, might say infant baptism); the priesthood of all believers will possibly be an important concept to some, while the freedom of the Holy Spirit in worship might be vital to others. Some people may say it's the simpler things like hospitality that are important to them; others may feel that theological concepts about the nature of the Eucharist have defining value. If you're using the cards, give each group a few and ask them to write the ideas down.

Call them to order and ask for some examples from the different groups. Someone might like to come forward and Blu-Tack the cards around the picture, or you could just ask them to call out while you write things up.

You should finish up with quite a list of what people regard as important aspects of faith, all clustered around Jesus or the cross. You can then simply point out that it is Christ who is truly central to our faith, and he draws together a whole variety of principles and ideas. This is shown in the Gospels in the story of the Transfiguration, in which the two main elements of Jewish scripture – the law and the prophets – are brought together in the presence of Christ and become focused on him.

Word: Mark 9:2-10
Moses, Elijah and Jesus

(See page 131 for a dramatised version of this story.)

There are some pretty strange stories in the Bible – and this is one of them. So, I want you to imagine we're back in the time when Jesus was living his earthly life. Now, see if you can work out where we are. The air's a bit on the cool side for the time of day; we're all a bit out of breath; and there's this incredible view – we can see for miles. So, where do you think we are?

OK, so we're up a mountain. Jesus has come up here with his closest friends, Peter, James and John. And he hasn't told them why. Perhaps we can hear them talking.

'I don't know what this is all about,' Peter's saying, 'but it'd better be good. I'm a seaman, I am – not a mountain man.'

James and John have probably got their own theories. We know James and John were a bit full of themselves – wanted to be the top people, and thought Jesus was going to give them power. We can just hear John saying, 'He's brought us up here to look at our kingdom, that's what. One day, we'll be in charge of all this – isn't that right, James?'

'You – in charge?' Peter scoffs. 'Jesus wouldn't put you two in charge of a compost heap – he's got more sense!'

Just a minute, though – what's happening? Jesus is starting to look really odd – his robe is starting to glow. And as we watch, it gets brighter and brighter, until it's shining so much it's dazzling to look at!

'All right,' we can hear James saying. 'If you're so all-fired clever, explain that.'

No one can, of course – but it's about to get even more weird. Suddenly there are two other men there, talking with Jesus. Not ordinary men – to be honest, they look a bit wild: they've got long beards, untidy hair, and clothes that most people certainly wouldn't wear to church, let alone to meet Jesus face to face – well, not without giving them a good ironing, anyway.

'It's Moses and Elijah!' James whispers.

'Of course it is,' says John. 'Anybody can see that.'

Now why it's so obvious isn't really – um – obvious, but they all seem agreed about it. The people talking with Jesus are Moses and Elijah. Now, Peter's always been one to get carried away – so you can imagine how he reacts. 'Hey, Teacher!' he says. 'Is this terrific, or is this terrific! Why don't we make three shelters here – one for you, one for Moses and one for Elijah? Then we could just stay here, all the time, couldn't we?'

The truth is poor old Peter's really as scared as everyone else and doesn't honestly know what to say – so instead of saying nothing he's saying anything – anything that comes into his head, without thinking about it first. Peter's trouble is he's got a mouth like a tumble dryer – he just opens it and whatever happens to be at the front falls out!

Anyway, back to the story. There they are, all pretty frightened and trying not to show it, when the whole scene gets even more spooky. I mean, on a clear day, when you can see for miles, suddenly there's this thick, black cloud. No rain – just a cloud, coming from nowhere – and it covers everybody. And then there's a voice – seems to come from the cloud itself. 'This is my Son,' it booms. 'This is the special one – pay attention to him.'

So, we've got Jesus, with his robes shining and glittering like disco lighting; we've got these two old guys – Moses and Elijah, who we all know have been dead for centuries; we've got a big, dark cloud; and we've got a voice coming from nowhere. What d'you make of all that, then?

Too late! It's gone! There's Peter with his face buried in the grass, pretending to be looking for grasshoppers but shaking and trembling as if it's going out of fashion, and James and John gazing around them with their mouths open – and Jesus, standing there all alone as if nothing's happened at all.

'Time to go,' Jesus says. 'We can't stay up here all the time – there's work to do.'

So, they start off down the mountain again, with James and John all agog to find out what it all meant.

'Come on, Jesus – what was all that about?' James is asking him.

'That's not for you to know at the moment,' Jesus says, mysteriously. 'And don't go blabbing about this to everyone else, either – got it? You can tell them all about it after I've risen from the dead.'

'Risen from the dead?' says Peter. 'Now, there's an idea – but what does it mean?'

And so they walk away, down the mountain again – gassing away among themselves, and leaving us to work out what it was all about.

Song 2

Offering

This may be introduced as symbolising our willingness, however imperfect, to offer ourselves fully to God, open to all that an experience of his love may hold.

Offertory prayer

Loving God, we offer you ourselves,
our lives, the things we hold dear,
for you to refine and use
so that the world may know your love.
Amen.

Song 3

Reading

Matthew 5:13-20 read from a standard Bible. Introduce it with words such as: Jesus emphasises that he has come not to abolish the great traditions, but to fulfil them.

Talk (optional)

If you feel it appropriate (and if time permits) you can reinforce the point that Jesus' whole life revealed the love which is at the heart of God's law, and which also drove the prophets to challenge injustice and corruption. This is not a love that smiles sweetly and avoids conflict; it's a love that cares so much that it hurts – and that cares enough to challenge all that is not for our well-being.

Notices and family news

Prayers of intercession

Song 4

Closing prayer/benediction

Dramatised reading
Moses, Elijah and Jesus

Narrator	Now, there are some pretty strange stories in the Bible – and this is one of them. So, I want you to imagine we're back in the time when Jesus was living his earthly life. Now, see if you can work out where we are. The air's a bit on the cool side for the time of day; we're all a bit out of breath; and there's this incredible view – we can see for miles. So, where do you think we are?
	OK, so we're up a mountain. Jesus has come up here with his closest friends, Peter, James and John. And he hasn't told them why. Perhaps we can hear Peter talking.
Peter	I don't know what this is all about, but it'd better be good. I'm a seaman, I am – not a mountain man.
Narrator	James and John have probably got their own theories. We know James and John were a bit full of themselves – wanted to be the top people, and thought Jesus was going to give them power. We can just hear what John might say.
John	He's brought us up here to look at our kingdom, that's what. One day, we'll be in charge of all this.
Peter	You two – in charge? Jesus wouldn't put you two in charge of a compost heap – he's got more sense!
Narrator	Just a minute, though – what's happening? Jesus is starting to look really odd – his robe is starting to glow. And as we watch, it gets brighter and brighter, until it's shining so much it's dazzling to look at!
James	All right, if you're so all-fired clever, explain that.
Narrator	No one can, of course – but it's about to get even more weird. Suddenly there are two other men there, talking with Jesus. Not ordinary men – to be honest, they look a bit wild: they've got long beards, untidy hair, and clothes that most people certainly wouldn't wear to church, let alone to meet Jesus face to face – well, not without giving them a good ironing, anyway.
James	It's Moses and Elijah!
John	Of course it is – anybody can see that.
Narrator	Now why it's so obvious isn't really – um – obvious, but they all seem agreed about it. The people talking with Jesus are Moses and Elijah. Now, Peter's always been one to get carried away – so you can imagine how he reacts.
Peter	Hey, Teacher! Is this terrific, or is this terrific! Why don't we make three shelters here – one for you, one for Moses and one for Elijah? Then we could just stay here, all the time, couldn't we?
Narrator	The truth is poor old Peter's really as scared as everyone else and doesn't honestly know what to say – so instead of saying

131

nothing he's saying anything – anything that comes into his head, without thinking about it first. Peter's trouble is he's got a mouth like a tumble dryer – he just opens it and whatever happens to be at the front falls out! Anyway, back to the story. There they are, all pretty frightened and trying not to show it, when the whole scene gets even more spooky. I mean, on a clear day, when you can see for miles, suddenly there's this thick, black cloud. No rain – just a cloud, coming from nowhere – and it covers everybody. And then there's a voice – seems to come from the cloud itself.

God   This is my Son. This is the special one – pay attention to him.

Narrator   So, we've got Jesus, with his robes shining and glittering like disco lighting; we've got these two old guys – Moses and Elijah, who we all know have been dead for centuries; we've got a big, dark cloud; and we've got a voice coming from nowhere. What d'you make of all that, then?

Too late! It's gone! There's Peter with his face buried in the grass, pretending to be looking for grasshoppers but shaking and trembling as if it's going out of fashion, and James and John gazing around them with their mouths open – and Jesus, standing there all alone as if nothing's happened at all.

Jesus   Time to go. We can't stay up here all the time – there's work to do.

Narrator   So, they start off down the mountain again, with James and John all agog to find out what it all meant.

James   Come on, Jesus – what was all that about?

Jesus   That's not for you to know at the moment. And don't go blabbing about this to everyone else, either – got it? You can tell them all about it after I've risen from the dead.

Peter   Risen from the dead? Now, there's an idea – but what does that mean?

Narrator   And so they walk away, down the mountain again – gassing away among themselves, and leaving us to work out what it was all about.

Festivals

Christmas

Preparation page

What's the point?

Shepherds got left out of everything in Bible days. They were unpopular (they weren't always fussy over whose land they led their sheep in search of pasture) and spent most of their time in a state of being ritually unclean. They were also physically isolated for much of their time, working unsocial hours in remote places. So, all ways round, they were not the people you'd expect to be at the top of God's guest list – they weren't even *on* anybody else's!

Preparation

Prepare the outfits and props for a simple role-play (see 'Action' in the All-age worship). These could be elaborate costumes or simple, representative props or badges – for example: a homeless beggar with a notice slung round the neck saying, '2 children to support' and a begging bowl in hand; an unemployed person could just carry a placard saying, 'Work wanted – cheap rates'; someone else could carry a notice saying, 'Fresh horse manure, £1 per bag'. (Perhaps you can think of other examples of people who would be less than welcome in many places.) The 'postie' simply needs a bag, a badge saying 'Royal Mail' and a letter to hand to the worship leader.

Suggested songs

Come and join the celebration
God was born on earth
Hee, haw! Hee, haw!
See him lying on a bed of straw
There's a star in the East (Rise up, shepherd, and follow)
While shepherds watched

Checklist

For the service, you will need:

- the props/costumes
- people to act the parts
- the letter for the 'postie' to hand over

All-age worship

Opening song

A song praising and celebrating the faithfulness of God

Prayer

Loving God,
we praise you for coming into the world and into our lives –
for caring about us enough to share with us in all our experiences.
We thank you for Jesus, who came to show us your love
in ways that still challenge us as well as fill us with joy.
Please forgive us for the times we forget how great your love is,
and when we treat some people as less important.
Help us to remember that everyone is important to you –
and especially, help us to remember, and to celebrate,
that that means us.
Thank you, Loving God, for all that this season means to us.
Amen.

Word and action

Action

Have the actors waiting out of sight, and start by telling the congregation that you're very excited because you're expecting a personal visit from Jesus himself. The first actor knocks, and you excitedly call, 'Come in', only to look disappointed when one of the actors enters and then immediately hustle him or her out again, saying something like, 'We don't want Jesus getting the wrong impression, do we?'

Repeat this, with slight variations until all the characters except the postie have been in. When the postie knocks and enters, you can look surprised – who would be sending you a letter on Christmas Day? Open the letter and read out:

Dear [*Your name*]

I'm so sorry to have embarrassed you by inviting my friends along – I thought you would be pleased, but I obviously misunderstood. So as to avoid causing you any more distress, I'll just go somewhere else – I really don't want to be any trouble.

All my love to you all,

Jesus.

PS Happy Christmas

Now you can act suitably chastened, and ask the actors to return before pointing out that all the time you were excitedly waiting for Jesus he was already here – but not in quite the form you were expecting!

Now, have the story read, in either narrative or dramatised form.

Word: Luke 2:8-20
God's gentle revolution

(See page 140 for a dramatised version of this story.)

Abi and Sam were shepherds, and they both wanted a change. 'It's not the job itself,' Sam said. 'I just don't like being looked down on all the time.'

Abi tried to encourage him. 'Don't worry, Sam,' she said, 'come the revolution *we'll* be calling the shots.'

'Oh, you and your revolution!' scoffed Sam. 'You've got to change people's *attitudes* – and no revolution is going to do that. No, shepherds have always been the bottom of the heap and we always will be. Face it, Abi – no one wants us, not nowhere, not nohow.'

'Now, what sort of a way is that to speak?' came a voice. 'Just because you're a shepherd doesn't mean you have to talk nonsense!' Abi and Sam stared in amazement; the speaker was about ten feet tall, in a long white robe with a pair of enormous wings and a ring of light around his head that lit up the entire night sky.

Abi and Sam threw themselves flat on the ground in fear. 'It's God, come to punish us,' Sam trembled. 'It's all your fault, going on about revolutions and things.'

'Well, if you didn't moan all the time . . .' Abi retorted.

'Oh, dear,' said the angel. 'I was afraid this would happen. That's the trouble with ceremonial dress, it frightens people. Look, I can't change in the middle of a mission – it's not allowed – but just don't be frightened, OK? I've got good news for you.'

Slowly, Abi and Sam raised their heads. 'Good news?'

The angel didn't look so terrifying any more – just impressive. 'Sure thing,' he said. 'Good news for you and for the whole world. It's about your Saviour – you know, the one everyone's been on about for centuries? Well, he's here – well, near here – in Bethlehem, to be exact.'

Abi was absolutely over the moon. 'That's it – it's started,' she crowed. 'Up the revolution!'

'Oh, you and your revolutions!' scoffed Sam. 'Don't you know a hallucination when you see one?'

The angel interrupted. 'Oh, it's true enough – you don't think I get all dolled up like this for just any old ceremony, do you? I mean, this is really mega – and I suppose it is a *kind* of revolution, but not the sort you're after. *You're* the ones God wants to be the first to know. He's chosen *you* to be the first visitors. I mean, the priests aren't even going to be told, and the king's being kept well in the dark – I'd say that was pretty revolutionary! Go to Bethlehem and look for a baby wrapped in strips of cloth and lying in a donkey's feeding trough. You don't get many of those to the postal district, so you'll know it's the right one.'

The angel raised his hands and snapped his fingers. 'Cue music!' Instantly, the night air was filled with the most wonderful singing – it was a kind of mixture of every different sort of music they'd ever heard – and quite a lot that they hadn't, as well. And for some reason, it all sounded great together! The angel raised his hand again. 'And . . . action!'

'Good grief!' exclaimed Abi. 'There's thousands of them!' And there were – angels stacked up as far as the eye could see, singing, dancing and generally making whoopee. 'Glory to God in heaven!' they thundered. 'Peace to his people on earth!' Peace? No chance of that, with all that racket! Strangely, though, the sheep didn't seem at all frightened – just went on chewing the grass as though nothing was happening.

Then Sam realised. 'No one else can hear it! It's just for us – all this is being laid on just for us.'

Abi was as amazed as Sam. 'They wouldn't allow that kind of stuff in the synagogue,' she said, as a troupe of angels did a conga across the horizon while another group rocked to the heavy beat of some instruments Sam and Abi had never seen before. Gradually, the music and the angels became more distant – their last sight was of the angel who'd talked to them high-kicking his way into the nearest cloud. 'Come on!' Sam gasped. 'Let's go to Bethlehem.'

Suddenly, minding the sheep didn't seem so important. They set off at the trot, expecting to find a party in full swing but when they got there, there were just the parents and the baby. Sam and Abi were awe-struck. 'So all that really was just for us!' said Sam. 'So much for not being important!'

Abi looked puzzled. 'I don't know what's going on,' she said, 'but I'm sure it's *some* kind of revolution.'

Song 2

Offering

This may be introduced as symbolising our response to the incredible love God shows us in coming to share our lives.

Offertory prayer

Holy God, as you offer yourself to us in simple ways,
so we bring our simple offering to you.
Help us so to offer ourselves and our gifts
that the world around us may recognise you
at the very heart of its life.
Amen.

Song 3

Reading

Isaiah 42:1-9 read from a standard Bible. Introduce it with words such as: Through the prophet Isaiah, God promises a Saviour whose rule will be based on gentleness and love, and yet he will radically transform the world.

Talk (optional)

If you feel it appropriate (and if time permits) you might point out that both the prophecy and the event were two-edged: gentle and comforting, yet radical and challenging. God does not merely comfort the oppressed, but exalts them – and that's going to be a threat to somebody else! So the gospel is not of a 'love' that's just nice to people, but a love that also challenges our assumptions and threatens to make a difference!

Notices and family news

Prayers of intercession

Song 4

Closing prayer/benediction

Dramatised reading
God's gentle revolution

Narrator	Abi and Sam were shepherds, and they both wanted a change.
Sam	It's not the job itself. I just don't like being looked down on all the time.
Abi	Don't worry, Sam – come the revolution *we'll* be calling the shots.
Sam	Oh, you and your revolution! You've got to change people's *attitudes* – and no revolution is going to do that. No, shepherds have always been the bottom of the heap and we always will be. Face it, Abi – no one wants us, not nowhere, not nohow.
Angel	Now, what sort of a way is that to speak? Just because you're a shepherd doesn't mean you have to talk nonsense!
Narrator	Abi and Sam stared in amazement; the speaker was about ten feet tall, in a long white robe with a pair of enormous wings and a ring of light around his head that lit up the entire night sky. Abi and Sam threw themselves flat on the ground in fear.
Sam	God's sent an angel to punish us. It's all your fault, going on about revolutions and things.
Abi	Well, if you didn't moan all the time . . .
Angel	Oh, dear, I was afraid this would happen. That's the trouble with ceremonial dress, it frightens people. Look, I can't change in the middle of a mission – it's not allowed – but just don't be frightened, OK? I've got good news for you.
Abi and Sam	Good news?
Narrator	The angel didn't look so terrifying any more – just impressive.
Angel	Sure thing. Good news for you and for the whole world. It's about your Saviour – you know, the one everyone's been on about for centuries? Well, he's here – well, near here – in Bethlehem, to be exact.
Abi	That's it – it's started! Up the revolution!
Sam	Oh, you and your revolutions! Don't you know a hallucination when you see one?
Angel	Oh, it's true enough – you don't think I get all dolled up like this for just any old ceremony, do you? I mean, this is really mega – and I suppose it is a *kind* of revolution, but not the sort you're after. *You're* the ones God wants to be the first to know. He's chosen *you* to be the first visitors. I mean, the priests aren't even going to be told, and the king's being kept well in the dark – I'd say that was pretty revolutionary! Go to Bethlehem and look for a baby wrapped in strips of cloth and lying in a donkey's feeding trough. You don't get many of those to the postal district, so you'll know it's the right one.
Narrator	The angel raised his hands and snapped his fingers.

Angel	Cue music!
Narrator	Instantly, the night air was filled with the most wonderful singing – it was a kind of mixture of every different sort of music they'd ever heard – and quite a lot that they hadn't, as well. And for some reason, it all sounded great together! The angel raised his hand again.
Angel	And . . . action!
Abi	Good grief! There's thousands of them!
Narrator	And there were – angels stacked up as far as the eye could see, singing, dancing and generally making whoopee.
Chorus	Glory to God in heaven! Peace to his people on earth!
Narrator	Peace? No chance of that, with all that racket! Strangely, though, the sheep didn't seem at all frightened – just went on chewing the grass as though nothing was happening. Then Sam realised.
Sam	No one else can hear it! It's just for us – all this is being laid on just for us.
Abi	[*Amazed*] They wouldn't allow that kind of stuff in the synagogue.
Narrator	As she spoke, a troupe of angels was doing a conga across the horizon while another group rocked to the heavy beat of some instruments Sam and Abi had never seen before. Gradually, the music and the angels became more distant – their last sight was of the angel who'd talked to them high-kicking his way into the nearest cloud.
Sam	Come on! Let's go to Bethlehem.
Narrator	Suddenly, minding the sheep didn't seem so important. They set off at the trot, expecting to find a party in full swing but when they got there, there were just the parents and the baby. Sam and Abi were awe-struck.
Sam	So all that really was just for us! So much for not being important!
Abi	I don't know what's going on, but I'm sure it's *some* kind of revolution.

Easter

Preparation page

What's the point?

The first people to learn about the resurrection are the women who stuck with Jesus all the way through. Often we feel like running away when life gets difficult – but if we run away from the pain, we're probably running away from the hope, too – because that's where it's going to be born!

Preparation

Prepare for an Easter procession. You will need a processional cross – if the church has one you might be able to use that, or if not make a simple one from two lengths of wood. Don't make it too big or heavy – for this service it needs to be clear that it isn't a burden but a symbol of liberation. Plan where the procession will go, and designate a child to lead it. If the route takes you through a few doors, that's all the better. This can be done very simply, or it could be made more powerfully symbolic if your building and resources are appropriate. For example, would your circumstances lend themselves to the idea of having some black curtains hung over the door leading out of the church? Another refinement would be to have a screen, using either a sheet of tissue-paper or just a few strips that could be taped across the doorway by which you will return – then you would be able to go through the dark curtains of 'death' and burst through the barrier on the way back, symbolising the breakthrough to new life! However simple or complicated you make it, keep the central point in mind: the journey to new life.

Suggested songs

Alleluia, alleluia, give thanks to the risen Lord
I danced in the morning
Sing a song, sing a joyful song
The women went to Jesus' tomb
This is the day, this is the day

Checklist

At the service, you will need:

- the processional cross
- a child to carry it and lead the procession
- perhaps a few stewards at key points along the route

All-age worship

Opening song

A song praising and celebrating the faithfulness of God

Prayer

Loving God, giver of all life and hope,
we praise and thank you this morning
for the wonderful news of Jesus' resurrection,
and for the promise that we too can have new life in him.
We thank you for giving us foretastes of that new life, here on earth,
and for the promise that we shall share it
in all its wonder and glory in eternity.
Forgive us for the times when we don't trust you enough,
and we shrink back from difficult steps that you are calling us to take,
and help us to trust in you for hope and renewal.
Through Jesus Christ our risen and living Lord.
Amen.

Word and action

Word: Luke 23:44-24:11
He's alive!

(See page 147 for a dramatised version of this story.)

Jesus' enemies thought they'd won when they saw him nailed to the cross, but they couldn't have been more wrong. Even there, Jesus showed that love can be stronger than hatred. He never cursed anyone – he even prayed for the people who were torturing him – and he comforted the criminal who was dying on the cross next to him. And the last words he said were words of faith. 'Father,' he said, 'I commend my soul into your care.'

Standing at the foot of the cross was a tough soldier – a hard man, who'd seen a lot of death – and even he couldn't help being impressed. 'What a man!' he said. 'He truly was a completely good man!'

Standing further away were some of the women who were friends of Jesus. They'd never left him, even at the most dangerous moments, but had stayed there to show they cared. 'You ought to go home,' said a passing man. 'This is no place for women.'

Joanna, one of the women, answered, 'Well, someone's got to be here to share his last moments with him – we're not going to let him die alone.' Then, when they knew Jesus was dead, she turned to Mary Magdalene and said, 'Let's go and see where they bury him – then we can come back later to pay our respects.'

Stealthily, not wanting to attract attention, they followed the men who were burying Jesus. They saw him placed hurriedly in a cave in the hillside, with a big stone rolled in front to seal it. 'After the religious festival's over,' said Mary, 'we'll come back and make sure he's given a *decent* burial.'

So it was that early on the Sunday morning, the same women – Joanna,

Mary Magdalene and the other Mary who was James's mother – all met with jars of spice and perfume to go to Jesus' grave. 'How are we going to move that big stone away from the grave?' asked Mary Magdalene.

'I don't know,' said the other Mary. 'Let's worry about that when we get there.'

'A lot of people would say were mad, anyway,' Joanna commented, 'but these things matter. Jesus always cared about other people, so now we're going to do the right thing by him.'

They walked silently in the early dawn light until they came within sight of the tomb, and they stopped in amazement and horror. 'Someone's opened it already,' gasped Joanna. 'The stone's been rolled away.'

'Someone's up to no good,' Mary Magdalene murmured quietly. 'Can't they just let him rest in peace?'

Slowly, they moved nearer to the tomb and peered in. It looked very spooky, but as their eyes got used to the low light they saw something that made them stop in amazement.

Nothing.

Jesus' body wasn't there.

They were staring open-mouthed at one another when suddenly the place was filled with light, and two men in dazzling white clothes stood in front of them. 'Why are you looking in a grave for someone who's alive?' one of them asked. 'Jesus isn't here – he's risen from the dead!' The women were terrified, but gradually the truth sank in as the man continued talking. 'Remember what he told you while he was with you before – how he'd be killed by his enemies but would rise again on the third day? Well, this is it!'

Suddenly, everything fell into place. Of course – God had raised Jesus to new life, just as Jesus had said that he would. The women didn't know whether to laugh or cry for joy!

'Fancy us being the first to know,' exclaimed Mary Magdalene.

'Not so surprising,' Joanna replied. 'After all, we stayed with him – and we're here now.'

'Come on!' cried the other Mary. 'We've got to tell the others.'

What a sight they were – stumbling over tree roots, tripping over the hems of their skirts, and laughing joyfully all the time, as they ran to where they knew the disciples were hiding. 'He's alive! He's alive! Really, he is – just as he promised he would be!'

At first, none of the men believed them – they thought the women had been dreaming or something. But they hadn't – and soon the whole world was going to be buzzing with the Good News: Jesus is alive!

Action

Explain to the congregation that you are going to invite them to follow the children in acting out the journey to new life. Everyone is invited to join in but if (as will almost inevitably be the case) there are those who would find it difficult, they are free simply to stay seated and use the time to pray for people who in real life are going through this experience. Now get the children to lead the procession, as you have planned it. If the procession is able to go outside the worship area of the church for a time, then perhaps you could arrange for the organist or music group to strike up a triumphant tune when they return.

Song 2

Offering

This may be introduced as a sign of our willingness to trust and follow God.

Offertory prayer

God of life,
we thank you for Jesus who offered his life for the world,
and now offers us new life.
Accept these gifts as tokens that we also offer our lives to you,
trusting you for hope and renewal.
Amen.

Song 3

Reading

Romans 8:11-17 read from a standard Bible. Introduce it with words such as: Paul tells the early Christians that the resurrection of Jesus is able to transform the lives we live here and now. New life, in this world!

Talk (optional)

If you feel it appropriate (and if time permits) point out that while at Easter the principal celebration is of true resurrection, we also celebrate the symbolic value of it – that God leads us through 'death' experiences to new life in the here and now – as, of course, the ancient Hebrews found out at the Red Sea! This is not to make light of the horrible experiences some people have in their lives, or to deny the reality of grief, but simply to hold to the hope that in the way he knows best God can lead us through these things.

Notices and family news

Prayers of intercession

Song 4

Closing prayer/benediction

Dramatised reading
He's alive!

Narrator	Jesus' enemies thought they'd won, when they saw him nailed to the cross, but they couldn't have been more wrong. Even there, Jesus showed that love can be stronger than hatred. He never cursed anyone – he even prayed for the people who were torturing him – and he comforted the criminal who was dying on the cross next to him. And the last words he said were words of faith.
Jesus	Father, I commend my soul into your care.
Narrator	Standing at the foot of the cross was a tough soldier – a hard man, who'd seen a lot of death – and even he couldn't help being impressed.
Soldier	What a man! He truly was a completely good man!
Narrator	Standing further away were some of the women who were friends of Jesus. They'd never left him, even at the most dangerous moments, but had stayed there to show they cared.
Passer-by (male)	You ought to go home. This is no place for women.
Joanna	Well, someone's got to be here to share his last moments with him – we're not going to let him die alone.
Narrator	Joanna was there with Mary Magdalene and another Mary, the mother of James, who all felt the same way. When they finally knew Jesus was dead, she turned to Mary Magdalene.
Joanna	Let's go and see where they bury him.
Mary Magdalene	Yes – then we can come back later to pay our respects.
Narrator	Stealthily, not wanting to attract attention, they followed the men who were burying Jesus. They saw him placed hurriedly in a cave in the hillside, with a big stone rolled in front to seal it.
Mary	After the religious festival's over, we'll come back and make sure he's given a *decent* burial.
Narrator	So it was that early on the Sunday morning, the same women – Joanna, Mary Magdalene and the other Mary – all met with jars of spice and perfume to go to Jesus' grave.
Mary Magdalene	How are we going to move that big stone away from the grave?
Mary	I don't know – let's worry about that when we get there.
Joanna	A lot of people would say were mad, anyway, but these things matter. Jesus always cared about other people, so now we're going to do the right thing by him.
Narrator	They walked silently in the early dawn light until they came within sight of the tomb, and they stopped in amazement and horror.

Joanna	Someone's opened it already. The stone's been rolled away.
Mary Magdalene	Someone's up to no good. Can't they just let him rest in peace?
Narrator	Slowly, they moved nearer to the tomb and peered in. It looked very spooky, but as their eyes got used to the low light they saw something that made them stop in amazement. Nothing. Jesus' body wasn't there. They were staring open-mouthed at one another when suddenly the place was filled with light, and two men in dazzling white clothes stood in front of them.
First man	Why are you looking in a grave for someone who's alive?
Second man	Jesus isn't here – he's risen from the dead!
Narrator	The women were terrified, but gradually the truth sank in as the men continued talking.
First man	Remember what he told you while he was with you before – how he'd be killed by his enemies but would rise again on the third day?
Second man	Well, this is it!
Narrator	Suddenly, everything fell into place. Of course – God had raised Jesus to new life, just as Jesus had said that he would. The women didn't know whether to laugh or cry for joy!
Mary Magdalene	Fancy us being the first to know!
Joanna	Not so surprising. After all, we stayed with him – and we're here now.
Mary	Come on! We've got to tell the others.
Narrator	What a sight they were – stumbling over tree roots, tripping over the hems of their skirts, and laughing joyfully all the time as they ran to where they knew the disciples were hiding.
Mary	He's alive! He's alive! Really, he is – just as he promised he would be!
Narrator	At first, none of the men believed them – they thought they'd been dreaming or something. But they hadn't – and soon the whole world was going to be buzzing with the Good News: Jesus is alive!

Pentecost

Preparation page

What's the point?

God's Holy Spirit gives his people the gifts they need in a particular time and place. For the early disciples, the gift of languages was vital – it enabled them to do God's work. We shouldn't expect that we'll all be given the same gifts, but in whatever way is best we believe God will empower us to do his work wherever we are.

Preparation

Make a model or picture of the world seen from space. This could be a simple picture, drawn or painted on paper and mounted for display, or it could be a more elaborate three-dimensional model, in which case you will need to find a way of standing it securely in the service. Then cut some flames from red and yellow card, not too large, but big enough to allow a few words to be written on each one. It might prove easiest to draw these on paper and then photocopy on to card and cut out – you will need enough for each group in the congregation to have a number of cards.

Suggested songs

Dance in your Spirit
I, the Lord of sea and sky
I'm enthusiastic
Oh! Oh! Oh! how good is the Lord
Spirit of love
The Spirit lives to set us free

Checklist

At the service, you will need:

- the picture or model of the world
- the flame cards
- some pens or pencils for the congregation
- Blu-Tack or pins

All-age worship

Opening song

A song praising and celebrating the faithfulness of God

Prayer

Lord God, we thank you for the gift of your Holy Spirit
to encourage and empower your people.
We pray that today you will lift our worship,
fill us with joy and hope,
and inspire us to spread your gospel.
Through Jesus Christ our Lord.
Amen.

Word and action

Word: Acts 2:1-12
The Spirit comes to those who wait

(See page 153 for a dramatised version of this story.)

You know, I never could work out what those people did in my back room. Oh, I'm Zedekiah, by the way, landlord of the Harp and Halo tavern in Jerusalem. Most people just call me Zed – because I snore a lot. Anyway, this bunch of people used to rent one of my rooms every weekend. They seemed a really odd lot to me, I don't mind telling you. Their leader was a man called Peter, and even he didn't seem to know what they were doing, but he had some really weird ideas, I can tell you.

'Well, we're just waiting, that's all,' he said.

'Waiting for what?' I asked.

'We don't know, but we'll know when it happens. Jesus told us to wait.'

Seemed potty to me. Oh, yes, and that was the other thing – this Jesus guy. Now, we all knew Jesus was dead, see – he'd been publicly executed weeks ago, and we'd all watched him die. Well, with no telly we have to get our entertainment somehow. But these friends of his were saying he'd risen from the dead and gone back to heaven to be with God. 'He's going to come back one day,' Peter insisted, 'and we've all got to make sure everyone's ready when he does. That's why we're waiting here – for him to give us the power.'

Well, it seemed to me they were quite capable of telling a tall story without any help from God's office, but they were harmless enough and they paid the rent, so I let them sit in my back room to wait for whatever-it-was – and whenever I had a few spare minutes I'd find an excuse to go and visit them. So there we all were, this one day – Pentecost, it was, which is our harvest festival, and you usually expect people to get a bit carried away then. But this wasn't hysteria, this was real – I was there, and I know. Thomas noticed it first. 'Hey,' he said, 'just listen to that wind.'

He was right – we could hear this roaring, rushing sound just like the big winds that come in off the desert – but it was different.

'Something creepy's happening,' said Philip. 'We can hear the wind, but nothing's being blown around.'

Mary Magdalene joined in next. 'I think this is it,' she said. 'I don't know what "it" is, but this is definitely it!'

Women! I ask you! Trouble is she turned out to be right, but it wasn't over yet. Suddenly, James started shouting, 'Don't panic! Don't panic – the room's on fire!'

Really odd, it was – there seemed to be flames all around us, touching each of the people there, but nothing was burning. And still we could hear that strange wind that no one could actually feel.

Peter flipped completely. 'Yippee!' he yelled, suddenly. 'It's happened! We've got the Power! The power of the Holy Spirit! Let's go tell everybody about Jesus.' And he was gone – just like that. Just like Peter, actually – he never did stop to think.

I tried to talk some sense into them, though. 'You can't just go out there spreading your stories,' I said. 'You need to think, plan, devise a corporate strategy. You've got to identify your consumer base.'

No one was listening. They'd all gone rushing out into the street. Well, I knew they were barking, but I really had to go and see what happened next – so I followed them outside. The first thing I heard was a Cypriot wine merchant talking.

'It's amazing! These are such ordinary people – I mean, they're just so, well, common, really. So how come they can talk to each of us in our own language?'

A Persian carpet-weaver scoffed. 'They're drunk, that's all it is!'

I was just going to tell him that if getting drunk made you fluent in five languages, most of my customers would earn a fortune as interpreters, but Peter got in first.

'Come off it!' he laughed. 'At this time of day? This is God's Spirit, not something out of a bottle – and it's being poured out on the whole world just as the prophet said it would be.'

Well, there was no holding them after that – soon everyone was hearing about Jesus. Even I ended up believing in him – just don't tell Peter, or I'll never hear the end of it.

Action

Divide the congregation into groups, giving a few cards to each group. They are going to put together a prayer list to set the world on fire! Ask them to discuss and write on the flames the gifts they would pray that the Holy Spirit will give to this church, to empower its mission, thinking of local issues as well as wider concerns. Assure them that their efforts will be taken seriously, and the cards later used to compile (or complement) a prayer calendar for the church. Examples might be: the gift of working with young people; the gift of encouragement to sustain people going through hard times; the gift of computer skills to enable the church to set up its own website; the gift of hospitality to welcome newcomers to the area –

and so on. Have a few such examples ready in case they need help, but don't jump the gun – you might get even better ideas from the groups if you don't steer them!

After a few minutes, call them back to order and ask what they have come up with. Let people come forward and, using Blu-Tack or whatever is suitable, stick the flames to the globe. Remind the congregation how these cards are going to be used, and then end the session with a short prayer for grace to wait expectantly.

Song 2

Offering

This may be introduced as symbolising the gifts the church already has which are being offered to God for renewal in his service.

Offertory prayer

Holy Spirit of God, inspire and inflame your church here,
that the gifts we offer and the gifts we hope to receive
may be used for the spreading of God's kingdom.
Through Jesus Christ our Lord.
Amen.

Song 3

Reading

1 Corinthians 12:27-13:7 read from a standard Bible. Introduce it with words such as: Paul tells us which, of all the gifts of the Holy Spirit, is the most important.

Talk (optional)

If you feel it appropriate (and if time permits) you could simply emphasise the point that the gifts God gives us are not for us to glorify ourselves, but to show his love to others and thus glorify him. One often hears the gifts talked about in very self-indulgent ways as if they were given to the church for its own benefit. But if love is the greatest gift, there must be a little more to it than that, mustn't there?

Notices and family news

Prayers of intercession

Song 4

Closing prayer/benediction

Dramatised reading
The Spirit comes to those who wait

Narrator	You know, I never could work out what those people did in my back room. Oh, I'm Zedekiah, by the way, landlord of the Harp and Halo tavern in Jerusalem. Most people just call me Zed – because I snore a lot. Anyway, this bunch of people used to rent one of my rooms every weekend. They seemed a really odd lot to me, I don't mind telling you. Their leader was a man called Peter, and even he didn't seem to know what they were doing, but he had some really weird ideas, I can tell you.
Peter	Well, we're just waiting, that's all.
Narrator	Waiting for what?
Peter	We don't know, but we'll know when it happens. Jesus told us to wait.
Narrator	Seemed potty to me. Oh, yes, and that was the other thing – this Jesus guy. Now, we all knew Jesus was dead, see – he'd been publicly executed weeks ago, and we'd all watched him die. Well, with no telly we have to get our entertainment somehow. But these friends of his were saying he'd risen from the dead and gone back to heaven to be with God.
Peter	He's going to come back one day, and we've all got to make sure everyone's ready when he does. That's why we're waiting here – for him to give us the power.
Narrator	Well, it seemed to me they were quite capable of telling a tall story without any help from God's office, but they were harmless enough and they paid the rent, so I let them sit in my back room to wait for whatever-it-was – and whenever I had a few spare minutes I'd find an excuse to go and visit them. So there we all were, this one day – Pentecost it was, which is our harvest festival, and you usually expect people to get a bit carried away then. But this wasn't hysteria, this was real – I was there, and I know. Thomas noticed it first.
Thomas	Hey, just listen to that wind.
Narrator	He was right – we could hear this roaring, rushing sound just like the big winds that come in off the desert – but Philip noticed that it was different.
Philip	Something creepy's happening. We can hear the wind, but nothing's being blown around.
Mary	I think this is it. I don't know *what* it is, but it's definitely it!
Narrator	Women! I ask you! But then, Mary Magdalene had always seemed a bit sus, to me. Trouble is she turned out to be right, in the end.
James	Don't panic! Don't panic – the room's on fire!
Narrator	James was in a right old state – but, to give him his due, it was pretty scary. There seemed to be flames all around us, touching each of the people there, but nothing was burning. And still

we could hear that strange wind that no one could actually feel. Peter flipped completely.

Peter Yippee! It's happened! We've got the Power! The power of the Holy Spirit! Let's go tell everybody about Jesus.

Narrator And he was gone – just like that. Just like Peter, actually – he never did stop to think. I tried to talk some sense into them, though. 'You can't just go out there spreading your stories,' I said. 'You need to think, plan, devise a corporate strategy. You've got to identify your consumer base.' But no one was listening. They'd all gone rushing out into the street. Well, I knew they were barking, but I really had to go and see what happened next – so I followed them outside. The first thing I heard was a couple of Cypriot wine merchants talking.

Cypriot 1 It's amazing! These are such ordinary people – I mean, they're just so, well, common, really. So how come they can talk to each of us in our own language?

Cypriot 2 They're drunk, that's all it is!

Narrator I was just going to point out that if getting drunk made you fluent in five languages, most of my customers would earn a fortune as interpreters, but Peter got in first.

Peter Come off it! At this time of day? This is God's Spirit, not something out of a bottle – and it's being poured out on the whole world just as the prophet said it would be.

Narrator Well, there was no holding them after that – soon everyone was hearing about Jesus. Even I ended up believing in him – just don't tell Peter, or I'll never hear the end of it.

Harvest: The parable of the talents

Preparation page

What's the point?

Contrary to popular opinion, the third servant wasn't denounced for failure but for not trying. The point was that he didn't trust his master enough to take the risk. Talents are like seeds – they have to be 'sown' if they are to increase. The other two servants experienced a kind of harvest – but only because they put at risk the resources they had.

Preparation

Cut some cards roughly in the shape of seeds and large enough for a few words to be written on them. Take a box such as a shoebox and decorate it to make it look special. Write on the front or on the lid: [*Name* of your church]: Seeds for Sowing.

Suggested songs

If I were a butterfly
Let us talents and tongues employ
Take my hands, Lord
We eat the plants that grow from the seed

Checklist

At the service, you will need:

- the seed cards
- the seed box
- some pens or pencils for the congregation

All-age worship

Opening song

A song praising and celebrating the faithfulness of God

Prayer

Loving God,
at this harvest festival we thank you for giving us seeds to sow,
and for helping them to grow into crops that we can use.
We thank you for the literal harvest of food,
by which we and others are fed.
We thank you also for that even greater harvest of your kingdom:
for the skills and resources you give us to use to your glory.
Please forgive us for the times
when we don't trust you enough to sow those seeds.
Help us to remember how great you are,
and to trust you for the harvest of our talents.
Amen.

Word and action

Word: Matthew 25:14-30
You mean you didn't even try?

(See page 160 for a dramatised version of this story.)

D'you know what a talent is – when people say, 'She's got a talent for singing'? I'm going to tell you how it came to be used that way. It started with a story Jesus told, at a time when 'talent' meant a kind of money – like a pound in Britain, or a dollar in America.

Bart was a rich man. He had a big business empire, selling everything from nails to nutcrackers, from feathers to furniture. Most things people wanted, Bart could provide – which was why he was rich.

Bart had to go away for a while, and thought it a good chance for some of his staff to show what they could do. So he called three of them to him. John was very bright, and could probably handle quite a big project. 'You can have five talents,' Bart told him.

'Five talents!' John exclaimed. 'That's a lifetime's wages to me. And I know just what to do with it.'

Then, Bart turned to Sarah. 'You can have two talents. With your imagination you should do well with that.'

Meanwhile, the third servant, Sam, was getting really worried. 'I don't want the responsibility,' he thought to himself. 'I'd rather stay as I am, thank you very much.'

'You can have one talent,' Bart said. 'I know you're not particularly energetic, but see what you can do with it.'

John wasted no time. He knew exactly where the opportunity lay. Bart's business sold most things people wanted, but John knew there were a lot of people who couldn't walk very well, or couldn't carry heavy things home. So he took on a team of people. 'Go out into the villages,' he said, 'and make a list of housebound people. Then you can visit them regularly, and do their shopping for them.'

Well, in no time at all, things were really buzzing. John had found a whole new group of people to sell to. And it gave the company a caring look, too, so other people who didn't need John's delivery service still shopped at Bart's because they liked to deal with a caring company.

Sarah had always wished she'd got a bit of money, because she wanted to invent something. Her mum, Mary, was getting old and her hands were weak. She'd always loved oranges, but now she couldn't enjoy them any more unless someone else peeled them for her – and always asking for help was embarrassing. Sarah knew there must be other people like her mum, and thought there must be a market for a really good orange peeler for people with weak hands. Well, this was her chance. She spent her two talents on developing her idea, taking each new version of the peeler home for her mother to try. After months of patient work, she'd got it right and Mary was back to enjoying her favourite fruit again. Sarah had just enough money left from her two talents to start production of her new orange peeler, and before she knew what was happening, John's sales team were coming in with orders for it from all the surrounding villages. Sarah had a winner on her hands.

And what of Sam – what was he doing with his one talent? 'Huh!' he thought. 'I don't want any part of this. I know what'll happen – it'll all go wrong and then I'll get the blame because I couldn't live up to Bart's high standards. Well, I'm not getting involved. I'll just keep the money safe.' So Sam dug a hole and put the money in it, to wait for Bart to come home.

'Well,' said Bart, 'what have you done with your talents?'

John beamed with pride. 'Here are your five talents – and five talents profit from my new scheme.'

'Wonderful!' Bart exclaimed. 'I'll make you a partner in my business! What about you, Sarah?'

Sarah was proud, too. 'Here are your two talents back,' she said, 'and two more – profits from my invention.'

'Great stuff!' Bart congratulated her. 'I'm making you a partner in my business, too.'

So what about Sam? Poor Sam! 'Well, it's like this,' he faltered. 'I, er, I knew what a great businessman you are – what high standards you set – and I didn't want to let you down. So I kept your money safe by burying it, and here's your one talent back.'

Bart was sad. 'Even if you failed,' he said, 'you could at least have tried. If nothing else, you could have put the money in the bank and got some interest. I'm really disappointed in you, Sam.'

Bart threw a party for John and Sarah, to celebrate their success. Poor Sam had nothing to celebrate, so he was left out. And that was a shame, because Bart wouldn't have punished him if he'd tried and failed. What hurt Bart was that Sam didn't trust him enough to take the risk.

Action

Divide the congregation into groups, ensuring that each group has a number of 'seeds'. Their task is to identify what 'talents' God has given to this church, and ways that they may be sown. Emphasise that you're not about press-ganging people to volunteer for jobs but are thinking in more general terms about the resources the church has; resources that could be 'sown' more liberally in the surrounding community and increase God's harvest.

If groups need help, you might have a few ideas up your sleeve. Is the church good at organising 'bun fights'? Does the building have useful features that the community could use better?

After a short time, call the groups back to order and ask people to share their ideas. Pass the shoebox round to collect the 'seeds' which will be passed either to the appropriate groups in the church for feeding into the church's mission.

Song 2

Offering

This may include the offerings of produce or other gifts that can be used as 'seed' – good clothes for a hostel for the homeless, or basic provisions for a disaster appeal (be sure to check what's really wanted, first). It may be introduced as a token recognition that all our 'harvests' – whether of crops, products, success, friendship or whatever – come from God and truly belong to him.

Offertory prayer

Thank you, loving God, for all your gifts.
Help us to recognise how, in sharing your gifts with others,
we sow seeds toward the great harvest of love, justice and peace
that is your kingdom.
May what we offer here, visible and invisible, be used to that end.
Amen.

Song 3

Reading

Leviticus 19:9-10 read from a standard Bible. Introduce it with words such as: In the Old Testament law, God warns us not to be greedy with the harvest he has given.

Talk (optional)

If you feel it appropriate (and if time permits) you can point out the implication that the resources the earth gives are not the sole property of those who exploit them but are given for the benefit of the whole creation. Apart from providing for the poor, this text is also about not wringing every last drop of profit from the environment.

Notices and family news

Prayers of intercession

Song 4

Closing prayer/benediction

Dramatised reading
You mean you didn't even try?

Narrator	D'you know what a talent is – like when people say, 'She's got a talent for singing'? I'm going to tell you how it came to be used that way. It started with a story Jesus told, at a time when 'talent' meant a kind of money – like a pound in Britain, or a dollar in America. Bart was a rich man. He had a big business empire, selling everything from nails to nutcrackers, from feathers to furniture. Most things people wanted, Bart could provide – which was why he was rich. Bart had to go away for a while, and thought it a good chance for some of his staff to show what they could do. So he called three of them to him.
Bart	John, you're very bright, and could probably handle quite a big project. You can have five talents.
John	Five talents! That's a lifetime's wages to me. And I know just what to do with it.
Bart	Sarah, you can have two talents. With your imagination you should do well with that.
Narrator	The third servant, Sam, was getting really worried.
Sam	I don't want the responsibility. I'd rather stay as I am, thank you very much.
Bart	Sam, you can have one talent. I know you're not particularly energetic, but see what you can do with it.
Narrator	John wasted no time. He knew exactly where the opportunity lay. Bart's business sold most things people wanted, but John knew there were a lot of people who couldn't walk very well, or couldn't carry heavy things home. So he took on a team of people.
John	Go out into the villages, and make a list of housebound people. Then you can visit them regularly, and do their shopping for them.
Narrator	Well, in no time at all, things were really buzzing. John had found a whole new group of people to sell to.
John	And it gave the company a caring look, too, so other people who didn't need my delivery service still shopped at Bart's because they liked to deal with a caring company.
Narrator	Sarah had always wished she'd got a bit of money, because she wanted to invent something.
Sarah	My mum, Mary, was getting old and her hands were weak. She'd always loved oranges, but now she couldn't enjoy them any more unless someone else peeled them for her – and always asking for help was embarrassing. I knew there must be other people like Mum, and thought there must be a market for a really good orange peeler for people with weak hands.

Narrator	Well, this was her chance. She spent her two talents on developing her idea, taking each new version of the peeler home for her mother to try. After months of patient work, she'd got it right and Mary was back to enjoying her favourite fruit again.
Sarah	I had just enough money left from my two talents to start production, and before we knew what was happening, John's sales team were coming in with orders for it from all the surrounding villages.
Narrator	So, Sarah had a winner on her hands. And what of Sam – what was he doing with his one talent?
Sam	Huh! I don't want any part of this. I know what'll happen – it'll all go wrong and then I'll get the blame because I couldn't live up to Bart's high standards. Well, I'm not getting involved. I'll just keep the money safe.
Narrator	So Sam dug a hole and buried the money, to wait for Bart to come home.
Bart	Well, what have you done with your talents?
John	Here are your five talents – and five talents profit from my new scheme.
Bart	Wonderful! I'll make you a partner in my business! What about you, Sarah?
Sarah	Here are your two talents back, and two more – profits from my invention.
Bart	Great stuff! I'm making you a partner in my business, too. What about you, Sam?
Sam	Well, it's like this: I, er, I knew what a great businessman you are – what high standards you set – and I didn't want to let you down. So I kept your money safe by burying it, and here's your one talent back.
Bart	That's really sad. Even if you failed, you could at least have tried. If nothing else, you could have put the money in the bank and got some interest. I'm really disappointed in you, Sam.
Narrator	Bart threw a party for John and Sarah, to celebrate their success. Poor Sam had nothing to celebrate, so he was left out. And that was a shame, because Bart wouldn't have punished him if he'd tried and failed. What hurt Bart was that Sam didn't trust him enough to take the risk.

Church Anniversary

Preparation page

What's the point?

We celebrate our life as a forgiven and forgiving community. It's worth reflecting that it's a good thing God's more forgiving than we are, because otherwise we'd be in real trouble . . .

Preparation

Divide the long edge of a piece of A4 paper into ten sections and the short edge into seven. You should end up with 70 'cells' each about 3 centimetres square. Photocopy this on to seven sheets of card – if you can find different colours of card it will make it more fun – and cut out the 490 pieces, storing them in a container ready for the service

Suggested songs

Brother, sister, let me serve you
God forgave my sin
Hear what God says
Make me a channel of your peace

Checklist

At the service, you will need:

- the 490 card fragments
- one or more willing children to scatter them

All-age worship

Opening song

A song praising and celebrating the faithfulness of God

Prayer

Loving God, we're here on this anniversary Sunday
to celebrate our life together –
a community both forgiven and forgiving.
Thank you for the constant love you show us
even when we don't deserve it.
Forgive us for the times when our community life doesn't reflect that,
and help us, as we look ahead to another year,
to let your love and your values show more clearly in our life together.
Through Jesus Christ our Lord.
Amen.

Word and action

Word: Matthew 18:21-34
Forgiven and unforgiving

(See page 167 for a dramatised version of this story.)

'I'll kill him!' Peter was yelling. 'If Andrew criticises my fishing just once more . . . That's the sixth time he's done it today.'

'All I said,' Andrew protested, 'was that he couldn't fish for compliments.'

'That's it!' shouted Peter. 'That's seven times – and I reckon forgiving anybody seven times is enough, don't you, Jesus?'

'Not by a long chalk,' Jesus replied. 'In fact I'd say more like, oh, let's see, seventy times seven.'

Peter was amazed. 'Seventy times seven? Well, that's . . . that's . . . well, it's a lot, anyway.'

'Four hundred and ninety, actually,' Matthew replied. 'Trust me – I'm an accountant.'

Peter had a very quick answer ready for that, but Jesus interrupted. 'God's way of doing things is like this,' he said. 'There was once a great king – right? And he had this servant who owed him a lot of money.'

'How much money?' Matthew asked, 'We've got to get these details right, you know.'

'Oh, let's say ten grand,' Jesus answered.

'Ten grand!' Andrew whistled.

'About a quarter of a million crispy cod burgers at today's prices,' Mary Magdalene chipped in. 'More if you have them without batter.'

Jesus looked patient. 'Do you want to hear this story or not?'

'Sorry, Jesus,' Peter apologised. 'I'm agog.'

'Exactly,' Andrew cut in. 'And gogs can't fish!'

'Are you going to listen?' said Jesus, quickly stepping in between Andrew and Peter. 'Or shall I go down to the sea and talk to the waves instead – they would listen. Now, if I have your attention: this slave – we'll call him Simon – he owed the king all this money and the king wanted it back.'

'I don't blame him,' said Matthew.

'With knobs on,' agreed Mary.

'So he called Simon,' Jesus went on, 'and said, "I want my money." Of course, he knew Simon hadn't even got the price of a pair of shoelaces, let alone ten grand. "Don't worry, Simon," he said. "You needn't pay." Then, just as Simon was breathing a big sigh of relief, he added, "I'll just sell you instead – and your wife and children, and your belongings."

'Well,' Jesus went on, 'Simon begged and he pleaded – you've never seen anything like it since that sending-off at the Jerusalem sports stadium in last year's cup final – remember? Well, Simon grovelled, and he cried, and kissed the king's feet and said he'd get the money somehow.'

'Yeah, yeah,' Matthew said, 'we've all heard that one before.'

Jesus glared. 'Are you telling this story, or am I? Anyway, the king was a kind old character really, so he forgave him. "You needn't pay me," he said, "Just forget about it."'

'I say,' said Andrew, 'what a nice king!'

'A *very* nice king,' agreed Mary.

'Don't get carried away,' grunted Matthew. 'It only happens in books.'

'I've not finished yet,' Jesus said. 'Simon went running off to tell his wife the good news, and on the way he met another servant who owed him the price of a bag of cod tails.'

'They're ten a penny,' Mary cut in.

'Well,' Jesus continued, 'you'd have thought it was millions, the way Simon grabbed him, and shook him, and demanded his money. Of course, the poor guy hadn't got it on him, so Simon had him put in prison and kept there until he paid everything.

'As you'd expect, when the king found out, he was furious. "I let you off a debt of ten grand," he reminded Simon, "and now you've been and gone and done this – so into prison you go until you've paid the ten grand." And he had him thrown into the cell.'

'Too right!' said Andrew.

'Deserved all he got,' Peter added.

'Ungrateful little wretch!' hissed Mary Magdalene.

'Fine,' Jesus smiled. 'So does this mean I can expect you lot to be civil to one another from now on?'

Action

Ask the congregation if they can possibly imagine how much forgiveness that story represents.

Then let one or two of the children run down the aisles scattering the bits of coloured paper over the congregation.

Now, let's see how long it takes for the congregation to collect up those pieces and hand them back. If it looks like taking an inordinate amount of time – or if some pieces have got into places that are difficult to reach without undue disruption – then you can simply say that the point has been made. That is just one person's forgiveness potential – can they imagine that multiplied by the number in the congregation? If we could meet Jesus even half way on this, there would be an awful lot of forgiveness in the air! The church would be littered with love!

Song 2

Offering

This may be introduced as our way of showing we want to be part of what God's about. We have received so much ourselves – forgiveness and other gifts, too – that we want to share it with others, and we symbolise that by our offering.

Offertory prayer

Heavenly Father, we thank you for the greatness of your love
which holds us together as a community of your people.
Accept the token we offer here,
as a sign of our desire to reflect your love
more and more in our life together.
Amen.

Song 3

Reading

1 John 4:7-11 read from a standard Bible. Introduce it with words such as: The Bible reminds us that the basis of our faith is not what we do but what God does. The love we show is part of our faith-response to God's grace.

Talk (optional)

If you feel it appropriate (and if time permits) you can point out that this is not 'cheap grace'. True forgiveness is hard for both sides, calling as it does for the real honesty which is only found where there is real love. You might like to sing the song, 'Let love be real'.*

Notices and family news

Prayers of intercession

Song 4

Closing prayer/benediction

* Found in *21st Century Folk Hymnal; Hymns Old and New, Complete Anglican*, or *Hymns Old and New, Liturgical*, or a copy may be obtained from Kevin Mayhew Ltd.

Dramatised reading
Forgiven and unforgiving

Peter	I'll kill him! If Andrew criticises my fishing just once more . . . That's the sixth time he's done it today.
Andrew	All I said was that Peter couldn't fish for compliments.
Peter	That's it! That's seven times – and I reckon forgiving anybody seven times is enough, don't you, Jesus?
Jesus	Not by a long chalk. In fact I'd say more like, oh, let's see, seventy times seven.
Peter	Seventy times seven? Well, that's . . . that's . . . well, it's a lot, anyway.
Matthew	Four hundred and ninety, actually. Trust me – I'm an accountant.
Peter	Yes, Matthew – and we all know about . . .
Jesus	Listen to me. God's way of doing things is like this. There was once a great king – right? And he had this servant who owed him a lot of money.
Matthew	How much money? We've got to get these details right, you know.
Jesus	Oh, let's say ten grand.
Andrew	Ten grand!
Mary	About a quarter of a million crispy cod burgers at beach market prices – more if you have them without batter.
Jesus	Do you want to hear this story or not?
Peter	Sorry, Jesus. I'm agog.
Andrew	Exactly – and gogs can't fish!
Jesus	Are you going to listen, or shall I go down to the sea and talk to the waves instead – they would listen. Now, if I have your attention, this slave – we'll call him Simon – he owed the king all this money and the king wanted it back.
Matthew	I don't blame him.
Mary	With knobs on.
Jesus	So he called Simon, and demanded his money.
King	I want my money.
Jesus	Of course, he knew Simon hadn't even got the price of a pair of shoelaces, let alone ten grand.
King	Don't worry, Simon, you needn't pay, I'll just sell you instead – and your wife and children, and your belongings.
Jesus	Well, Simon begged and he pleaded – you've never seen anything like it since that sending-off at the Jerusalem sports stadium in last year's cup final – remember? Simon grovelled, and he cried, and kissed the king's feet and said he'd get the money somehow.

Matthew	Yeah, yeah, we've all heard that one before.
Jesus	Are you telling this story, or am I? Anyway, the king was a kind old character, really, so he forgave him.
King	You needn't pay me. Just forget about it.
Andrew	I say, what a nice king!
Mary	A very nice king.
Matthew	Don't get carried away – it only happens in books.
Jesus	I've not finished yet. Simon went running off to tell his wife the good news, and on the way he met another servant who owed him the price of a bag of cod tails.
Mary	They're ten a penny.
Jesus	Well, you'd have thought it was millions, the way Simon grabbed him, and shook him, and demanded his money. Of course, the poor guy hadn't got it on him, so Simon had him put in prison and kept there until he paid everything. As you'd expect, when the king found out, he was furious.
King	I let you off a debt of ten grand and now you've been and gone and done this – so into prison you go until you've paid the ten grand.
Andrew	Too right!
Peter	Deserved all he got.
Mary	Ungrateful little wretch!
Jesus	Fine! So does this mean I can expect you lot to be civil to one another from now on?

Remembrance Sunday: Cain and Abel _____

Preparation page

What's the point?

Cain interprets God's rejection of his gift as a rejection of himself, and takes out his wounded pride on his brother. Childish, of course, but not particularly unusual. Whether on an individual or a national scale, the result is often all too predictable.

Preparation

Prepare a 'bran tub' for a lucky dip – perhaps several if the congregation is large. Plastic buckets full of clean sawdust are probably the simplest method – they need to be small enough and light enough for children to pass around the congregation. In the sawdust conceal a number of simple prizes, but also some booby prizes – things that no one is likely to want: an old bottle top, an empty aerosol, for example.

Suggested songs

God said, 'Cain, where is your brother?'*
Make me a channel of your peace
Some things make you angry
When I needed a neighbour

Checklist

At the service, you will need

- the brantub(s)

---

* Written specially for this passage, this song can be found in *Wake up, world!* (Kevin Mayhew, 1993).

All-age worship

Opening song

A song praising and celebrating the faithfulness of God

Prayer

Loving God,
on this Remembrance Sunday, we come to honour
those who have died to preserve the freedom we enjoy.
We want to honour them in the best way we possibly can –
by building the peace they died for.
Help us to learn to see other people not as rivals
but as brothers and sisters,
and ensure that the great sacrifice made by countless people
will not be in vain.
Amen.

Word and action

Action

Tell the congregation about the lucky dip, but emphasise that the game depends on complete honesty. If they like what they get, they can accept it graciously; if they don't want it, they must be honest and politely put it back into the tub. If they don't want to take part in the game at all, they must be equally honest.

Let the children go round the congregation with their tubs, offering them to members of the congregation. After a short time, when there have been a number of refusals as well as acceptances, draw the game to a close and call the children back to the front. Ask the people who refused how they felt about refusing. Were they embarrassed? Were they reluctant to offend the children? Were they afraid of seeming ungrateful? Did anyone actually accept something they didn't want, despite your injunction to the contrary? If so, you can assume a tone of mock severity and have a bit of fun.

Now ask the children how they felt when people refused. Did they feel it was a personal rejection? If anyone has owned up to accepting what they didn't want, did the child guess? If so, what did they think?

The point is simple. Rejecting the gift is not the same as rejecting the giver. Too often, we feel hurt because our work or our gifts are not appreciated – and we take it personally. That can lead to all kinds of trouble. It also applies on a national scale. More than one over-sensitive politician has felt personally rejected and uttered the infamous words, 'This means war!'

Now you're going to hear a story about this from the Bible.

Word: Genesis 4:1-16
I am my brother's brother

(See page 174 for a dramatised version of this story.)

Adam and Eve (remember them – the first people God made?) – well, they had a couple of sons called Cain and Abel. Now, of course, all brothers and

170

sisters quarrel occasionally, but with Cain and Abel it was a way of life. Whatever one of them said, the other would disagree just for the sake of it, and before the next sparrow chirped there'd be tears and tantrums.

'I worry about those two,' said Eve. 'One day, one of them's going to draw blood.'

'Oh, I don't think so,' Adam answered. 'They've never been any good at art. But I'm seriously afraid one of them might get hurt if they don't stop quarrelling.'

Before Eve could reply, there were raised voices on the terrace. 'You give me that back – it's mine.'

'You haven't played with it for ages.'

'Well, I want to now.'

'Well, you can't, so there.'

Now, if you're hoping they'd grow out of this silliness, you've got another think coming. The words changed, but it was essentially the same argument.

'You've ruined my cabbage crop!' Cain roared at Abel. 'You and those lousy sheep of yours.'

'Well, where are they supposed to graze?' bellowed Abel. 'You've planted crops on every inch of land, you greedy parasite, and there's nothing left for me to use.'

'Don't call me a parasite.'

'I'll call you whatever I want.'

'No, you won't.'

'Yes, I will.'

And so it went on, until they'd completely forgotten what the real argument was about.

The day came when Abel – who, as you may have gathered, was a shepherd – decided to give God a present. 'The very best lamb I've got,' he said. 'Only that will be good enough for God.'

When Cain heard about it, he was hopping mad. 'Trying to get God on his side, is he?' he seethed. 'I'll show him what crawling's really about.' He gathered the best fruit and vegetables from his crops – and took them to where Abel was praying. 'There you are, God!' he crowed. 'Better than a pathetic little lamb, eh? Just so that you know, I'm your man – I'm the one to back around this joint. OK?'

God wasn't pleased. 'Is this what you think it's all about?' he demanded. 'Trying to get me on your side? Well, I'm happy with Abel's gift, thank you very much – he's being honest. And don't glower at me like that, either – I don't frighten that easily. Look, Cain, I'd get a grip on that temper if I were you, while you still can.'

'Yeah, yeah, I know,' sneered Cain and stormed off. Later, he said to Abel, 'Fancy a walk in the fields?'

Abel should have known better. He went off with Cain and guess what – next thing Abel knew, he was dead. Cain's temper had finally got the better of him. As Cain was walking home, wondering what to say to Adam and Eve, he heard God's voice.

'Hi, Cain – where's Abel?'

'What am I?' Cain sulked, 'my brother's keeper?'

'I know what you've done,' God said. 'I can hear his very blood crying out from the ground for justice – the same ground you expect to give you crops to eat, now fouled with your own brother's blood. Well, that's the end of all that. You're a man on the run now.'

'I can't run anywhere,' said Cain. 'Anyone who finds me will kill me.'

God sounded really stern now. 'Oh, no, death's too easy a way out for you,' he said. 'I'll make sure you have to live with this for a long time. Now go.'

So Cain ended up in the land of Nod. Oh, don't get me wrong – sleep wasn't part of the deal, not with Cain's conscience. Nod was the name of another country.

That's where Cain went, and that's where our story ends. Because no one has ever heard any more of either Cain or Nod since that time.

Silence

A time to remember, and to recommit ourselves to peace.

Song 2

Offering

This may be introduced as symbolic of our recognition of how much has been sacrificed for us, and our willingness to offer whatever we may of ourselves for a more peaceful world.

Offertory prayer

Holy God, we thank you for all you have sacrificed for us,
and today in particular all that others have given
that we might live in freedom.
In gratitude and penitence, we offer you ourselves and our gifts,
that the true memorial of lasting peace may be built in your world.
Amen.

Song 3

Reading

Isaiah 2:2-5 read from a standard Bible. Introduce it with words such as: Isaiah makes a direct connection: learning God's ways means renouncing war.

Talk

Emphasise that this is not to demean the courage of those who have died in wars, and neither does it in any way detract from their honoured memory. On the contrary: to commit ourselves to seeking true peace is the best – the only – way truly to honour them and what they did. The emphasis in the reading is first on seeking to know God's ways and then, as a direct consequence of that, making war redundant. As Christians we must surely have the faith to believe it is possible!

Notices and family news

Prayers of intercession

Song 4

Closing prayer/benediction

Dramatised reading
I am my brother's brother

Narrator	Adam and Eve (remember them – the first people God made?) – well, they had a couple of sons called Cain and Abel. Now, of course, all brothers and sisters quarrel occasionally, but with Cain and Abel it was a way of life. Whatever one of them said, the other would disagree just for the sake of it, and before the next sparrow chirped there'd be tears and tantrums.
Eve	You know, Adam, I worry about those two. One day, one of them's going to draw blood.
Adam	Oh, I don't think so, Eve. They've never been any good at art. But I'm seriously afraid one of them might get hurt if they don't stop quarrelling.
Abel	You give me that back – it's mine.
Cain	You haven't played with it for ages.
Abel	Well, I want to now.
Cain	Well, you can't, so there.
Narrator	Now, if you're hoping they'd grow out of this silliness, you've got another think coming. The words changed, but it was essentially the same argument.
Cain	Abel, you've ruined my cabbage crop – you and those lousy sheep of yours.
Abel	Well, where are they supposed to graze? You've planted crops on every inch of land, you greedy parasite, and there's nothing left for me to use.
Cain	Don't call me a parasite.
Abel	I'll call you whatever I want.
Cain	No, you won't.
Abel	Yes, I will.
Narrator	And so it went on, until they'd completely forgotten what the real argument was about. The day came when Abel – who, as you may have gathered, was a shepherd – decided to give God a present.
Abel	The very best lamb I've got. Only that will be good enough for God.
Narrator	When Cain heard about it, he was hopping mad.
Cain	Trying to get God on his side, is he? I'll show him what crawling's really about.
Narrator	Cain gathered the best fruit and vegetables from his crops – and took them to where Abel was praying.
Cain	There you are, God! Better than a pathetic little lamb, eh? Just so that you know, I'm your man – I'm the one to back around this joint. OK?

Narrator   God wasn't pleased.

God   Is this what you think it's all about? Trying to get me on your side? Well, I'm happy with Abel's gift, thank you very much – *he's* being honest. And don't glower at me like that, either – I don't frighten that easily. Look, Cain, I'd get a grip on that temper if I were you, while you still can.

Cain   Yeah, yeah, I know.

Narrator   Cain stormed off for a good sulk, and hatched a horrible plot.

Cain   Hey, Abel, fancy a walk in the fields?

Narrator   Abel should have known better. He went off with Cain and guess what – next thing Abel knew, he was dead. Cain's temper had finally got the better of him. As Cain was walking home, wondering what to say to Adam and Eve, he heard God's voice.

God   Hi, Cain – where's Abel?

Cain   What am I – my brother's keeper?

God   I know what you've done. I can hear his very blood crying out from the ground for justice – the same ground you expect to give you crops to eat, now fouled with your own brother's blood. Well, that's the end of all that. You're a man on the run now.

Cain   I can't run anywhere – anyone who finds me will kill me.

God   Oh, no – death's too easy a way out for you. I'll make sure you have to live with this for a long time. Now go.

Narrator   So Cain ended up in the land of Nod. Oh, don't get me wrong – sleep wasn't part of the deal, not with Cain's conscience. Nod was the name of another country. That's where Cain went, and that's where our story ends. Because no one has ever heard any more of either Cain or Nod since that time.